Popular Mechanics

MONEYSMART MAKEOVERS

PORCHES, DECKS & PATIOS

RICK PETERS

HEARST BOOKS
A division of Sterling Publishing Co., Inc.

New York / London
www.sterlingpublishing.com

Produced by How-2 Media Inc.
Design: Triad Design Group
Cover Design: Celia Fuller
Photography: Christopher J. Vendetta
Contributing Writer: Cheryl A. Romano
Cover Photo: Brown Jordan (www.brownjordanfurniture.com)
Back Cover photos: California Redwood Association (top right), Brown Jordan (www.brownjordanfurniture.com) (bottom left)
Spine photo: Brown Jordan (www.brownjordanfurniture.com)
Illustrations: Triad Design Group
Copy Editor: Barbara McIntosh Webb
Page Layout: Triad Design Group
Index: Nan Badgett

Library of Congress has catalogued the hardcover edition as follows:
Peters, Rick.
    Popular Mechanics moneysmart makeovers. Porches, decks & patios / Rick Peters.
        p. cm.
    Includes index.
    ISBN 1-58816-397-0
    1. Decks (Architecture, Domestic)—Design and construction—Amateurs' manuals. 2. Patios—Design and construction—Amateurs' manuals. 3. Porches—Design and construction—Amateurs' manuals. I. Title: Porches, decks & patios. II. Popular mechanics (Chicago, Ill. : 1959) III. Title.

TH4970.P4735 2005
690.893—dc22
                    2005046306

10 9 8 7 6 5 4 3 2 1

First Paperback Edition 2008
Published by Hearst Books
A Division of Sterling Publishing Co., Inc.
387 Park Avenue South, New York, NY 10016

Popular Mechanics and Hearst Books are trademarks of Hearst Communications, Inc.

www.popularmechanics.com

For information about custom editions, special sales, premium and corporate purchases, please contact Sterling Special Sales Department at 800-805-5489 or specialsales@sterlingpublishing.com.

Distributed in Canada by Sterling Publishing
c/o Canadian Manda Group, 165 Dufferin Street
Toronto, Ontario, Canada M6K 3H6

Distributed in Australia by Capricorn Link (Australia) Pty. Ltd.
P.O. Box 704, Windsor, NSW 2756 Australia

Manufactured in China

Sterling ISBN 13: 978-1-58816-684-5
    ISBN 10: 1-58816-684-8

Acknowledgments

For all their help, advice, and support, I offer special thanks to:

Angela Ross of TimberTech, for the beautiful composite decking, ornamental rail system, posts, and copper caps used for the high-end deck makeover.

Karla Neely of Thompson's Water Seal Products, for their fine deck cleaner and stain, used for the economy deck makeover.

Ken Gidney of Durable Deck, for the handsome deck cover materials used in the mid-range deck makeover.

Kathy Ziprick with Style Solutions, for supplying lightweight and easy-to-install urethane foam moldings and ornamentation used in the economy porch makeover.

Craig Weaver with ODL, Inc., for supplying the handsome, high-quality door glass used in the high-end deck and porch makeovers.

Karla Biddle of the Biddle Outdoor Center in Sedona/Prescott, Arizona, for the superb patio furniture and accessories, plus decorating expertise, used in all three of the patio makeovers.

Christopher Grover of the California Redwood Association, for the beautiful photographs of redwood decks, and technical information.

Steven Bean of the Southern Pine Council/Southern Forest Products Association, for the inspiring images of pine decks and porches, and technical information.

Stuart Hanson of the Western Red Cedar Lumber Association, for the stunning photographs of cedar decks, and technical information.

Lisa Sharp of Brown Jordan, for the gorgeous outdoor furniture images used throughout the book.

Christopher Vendetta, for taking great photographs under less-than-desirable conditions and under tight deadlines.

Rob Lembo and the crew at Triad Design Group, for superb illustrations and layout skills, whose talents are evident on every page of this book.

Barb Webb, copyediting whiz, for ferreting out mistakes and gently suggesting corrections.

Heartfelt thanks to my constant inspiration: Cheryl, Lynne, Will, and Beth.

Contents

Introduction

Does your deck seem dull? Is your porch looking pooped? Could your patio use more pizzazz? If a makeover is in order, you have lots of company: More and more homeowners are pushing their inside living spaces outdoors. As climate permits, we relish outdoor leisure. And as budgets permit, we want our surroundings to be comfortable and attractive.

MoneySmart Makeovers: Porches, Decks & Patios shows you the real-world options that you have to upgrade your outdoor spaces. Want to improve your deck without ripping up boards? We'll show you how. Looking for a more finished look for your front porch? Ways to beautify an old concrete patio? They're all here, and all focused on getting the most for your money.

Our subject homes aren't zillion-dollar "cottages," but real residences lived in by real people with real budgets. We take three outdoor spaces—a deck, a porch, and a patio—and make each one over three times. This way, you can see what's possible at three spending levels: economy, mid-range, and high-end, totaling nine different makeovers.

To help you reach your makeover goals, the book is divided into three parts. The "Planning a Makeover" section includes the fundamentals of construction and materials. In "Real Makeover Examples," you'll see the real-life deck, porch, and patio, and the three makeovers for each. And in "Creating a New Look," you'll go step by step through the basics that let you actually do the projects yourself.

Here's to a successful—and money-smart—makeover in your own great outdoors.

—James Meigs
Editor-in-Chief, *Popular Mechanics*

Planning Your Makeover

When it comes to home improvement, no one ever says, "Gee, I guess I should have planned less." The need for planning ahead certainly holds for decks, porches, and patios. Some might say that these outdoor spaces demand extra planning. Not only are they highly visual aspects of the home, but ignoring certain rules of construction (and sometimes building code) can undo all your plans.

In this section, we'll give you an inside look at what makes these outdoor spaces work (or not): The key areas are design, choosing materials, and systems. Your makeover might be as simple as painting a concrete slab—or as elaborate as transforming a deck into an outdoor dining room, complete with overhang. Whatever your plans, you'll find the basics you need to know in the following pages.

Does your outdoor space need a little work, or a lot of help? Either way (or anything in between), you'll find the money-smart solutions here.

DECK, PORCH & PATIO DESIGN

What's your style in outdoor space? Are you a redwood deck person? Is a rocking-chair country porch more your style? How about a party-ready patio just waiting for that next get-together? Whatever you have now, the first step in getting what you want is to know what's available.

If you haven't kept up with the latest innovations, you may be surprised to find how many choices you have for your makeover. New materials and techniques may give you more leeway in your budget and your design than you thought. On the other hand, the realities of construction may nudge you away from one idea and toward another. So before you begin, let this chapter introduce you to the styles and types of decks, porches, and patios waiting for your consideration. You may be convinced to stick to your original plan, or inspired to try something new.

DECK STYLES

Decks are grand spaces and cozy places, tiered, raised, freestanding, and attached. They're made of pine, redwood, cedar, and composites. They're wide open and private, usher you to a stunning view, and shield you from neighbors' eyes. Decks are all these things, depending on the home, the site, and the owner's personal style. Unlike interior spaces, which usually stick to an overall look, decks can bend the rules because they're a bridge between indoors and outdoors. So, a deck can either complement or contrast with a home's style. With accessories like railings and planters, a plain deck can become a visual pleasure.

Classic deck. Think "deck" (top right), and this is the image that frequently comes to mind. Classic, raised decking of pine transitions from the home to the yard, offering some privacy, accented with shrubs and flowers.

Clean and simple. The beauty of redwood (above) carries the clean, simple lines of this open-air deck. Steps away from the dining area, bench seating invites you to feel the sun's warmth or watch the moon rise.

Task-specific. The indoors comes outside with this outdoor kitchen, part of a sleek, task-specific redwood deck (left). Note the built-in lighting atop the cooking surface for safe meal preparation, anytime of day or night.

Contemporary. Clean, uncluttered, and contemporary: That's the effect of this entire deck space (above). A mix of concrete block and glass block in the privacy wall keeps it visually interesting, while beautiful redwood offers a warm, enduring contrast.

Private. Open, yet private: No contradiction of terms here, in a cedar enclosure (above) that many would envy. The slatted overhead lets in light while filtering the full sun, and the bountiful plants give it the feel of an indoor garden.

Sleek and elegant. Nothing short of "wow," this deck color really pops (left). Highly finished redwood has a rich, gleaming color on its own. Add the contrast of a bright painted railing, posts, and risers, and the wood itself becomes the focal point of this elegant design.

DECK TYPES

Most decks can be categorized into one of five broad types: freestanding, attached, single-level, raised, and multi-level. The type of deck you're making over will have an impact on what you can do and what types of materials you can use. For example, most composite decking products require at least 12" of ground clearance; this means they wouldn't be suitable for a low or ground-level deck (for more on composites, see page 31).

Freestanding deck. The simplest type of deck is the freestanding deck (often referred to as a grade-level deck), as shown in the top photo. Since this style deck does not attach to the house, it's really a wooden patio. This greatly simplifies construction since the deck usually rests directly on concrete piers. As the ground freezes, thaws, and refreezes, the entire deck moves up and down as a unit—something that won't happen when one part of the deck is attached to the house. Although you can find this style deck in a backyard, you'll most often find one in a remote location, such as near the edge of a lake or pond, or in a remote area of a property.

Attached deck. Most people want a deck that attaches to the home: It provides access in and out, and makes it easy to carry food and drinks back and forth. In an attached deck (like the one in the middle photo), one or more sides of the deck attach to the house via a structural member called a ledger (page 50). The other end or ends of the deck are supported by a beam-and-post arrangement. Since the end of the deck that's attached to the house remains in a fixed position, the opposite end must also remain fixed to prevent straining the foundation. That's why footings that support the beams and posts must be below grade (page 49). If they're not, the unattached end will rise and fall as the ground freezes and will eventually tear the deck apart.

Single-level deck. Single-level decks establish a transition between a house and a yard. For the smoothest possible transition, this style deck (bottom photo) often does not incorporate a railing system. Single-level decks are often simple rectangles, but can also feature curved edges. These decks also work well as wraparound decks that follow the shape of the house.

Raised deck. Next to the single-level attached deck, the raised or elevated deck—like the one shown in the top photo—is the most commonly built style. This type of deck stands on posts anywhere from 1 to 10 feet or higher—basically whatever it takes to reach the main level of the home—or the second level, if desired. One end of the raised deck attaches to the home via a ledger (see page 50); the other end is supported by a post-and-beam structure (see page 51). Because of this setup, raised decks are the solution to dealing with sloping ground and can also handle the varying floor plan of a split-level home.

Multi-level deck. Multi-level decks are by far the most complicated of all the deck styles, but they also afford the greatest design possibilities. Multi-level decks can handle steep slopes: The deck is divided into different levels that step up or down the slope to hug it more closely, as shown in the bottom photo. This style deck also lends itself to defining activity areas, such as a barbecue or pool area. Although a multi-level deck is basically two or more smaller decks joined together, this style deck should always be designed and modified by a professional, especially on those sites with steep slopes.

DECKING PATTERNS

The most visible part of the deck is the decking or deck boards. In most cases, the boards run parallel to the house (also called horizontal) and attach directly to the foundation. Depending on the visual effect desired, you can install a variety of patterns, such as diagonal right or left, V-shape (or parting board), herringbone, or vertical (see the drawing below). It's important to note that the more complicated the pattern, the more work it will require—not only in laying the decking, but also in building the appropriate foundation.

Diagonal. A diagonal pattern is one of the simplest variations, requiring only a modest amount of extra work, primarily in cutting the deck boards at an angle. This pattern can use the standard foundation you'd build for a standard parallel decking.

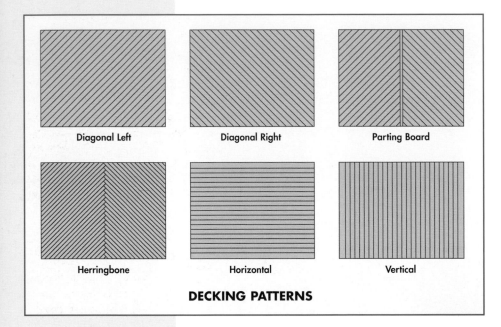

Diagonal Left	Diagonal Right	Parting Board
Herringbone	Horizontal	Vertical

DECKING PATTERNS

Parting board. A V-shape or parting board pattern is the next step up in visual interest. The only added work needed for the foundation is to add a double joist where the deck boards intersect. This extra joist provides added surface for nailing or screwing the deck boards in place. There's also slightly more work needed to cut the angles on the ends of the boards, since you'll have basically twice as many cuts as when installing a diagonal pattern.

Herringbone. Of all the decking patterns, the interlocking deck boards of a herringbone pattern offer one of the most pleasing deck patterns. But, this extra visual interest means more work. This pattern requires double field joists wherever the pattern interlocks to provide adequate fastening surfaces. Although the number of angled cuts is fewer than with some of the other patterns, the pattern itself is complicated and requires a lot of thought and advance planning.

Vertical. This simple-looking pattern also requires much additional framing work, as the decking runs parallel to the joists. The best way to produce this pattern is to run the joists parallel to the house. You'll need one or more beams to support the joists. Consult your local building inspector for more on this type of deck foundation.

DECK GUIDELINES

MAXIMUM JOIST SPACING

Species	Joist Size	12" O.C.	16" O.C.	24" O.C.
Douglas Fir – Larch	2×6	10' 9"	9' 9"	8' 1"
	2×8	14' 2"	12' 7"	10' 3"
	2×10	17' 9"	15' 5"	12' 7"
	2×12	20' 7"	17' 10"	14' 7"
Douglas Fir – South	2×6	9' 9"	8' 10"	7' 9"
	2×8	12' 10"	11' 8"	10' 0"
	2×10	16" 5"	14' 11"	12' 2"
	2×12	19" 11"	17' 4"	14' 2"
Hemlock-Fir	2×6	10' 0"	9' 1"	7' 11"
	2×8	13' 2"	12' 0"	10' 2"
	2×10	16' 10"	15' 2"	12' 5"
	2×12	20' 4"	17' 7"	14' 4"
Spruce-Pine-Fir	2×6	9' 6"	8' 7"	7' 6"
	2×8	12' 6"	11' 4"	9' 6"
	2×10	15' 11"	14' 3"	11' 8"
	2×12	19' 1"	6"	13' 6"
Western woods	2×6	9' 2"	8' 4"	7' 0"
	2×8	12' 1"	10' 10"	8' 10"
	2×10	15' 4"	13' 3"	10' 10"
	2×12	17' 9"	15' 5"	12' 7"

Since this book is about deck makeovers and not deck building, you might wonder why we've included some deck guidelines here. The reason is simple: It's important to know how your deck was built in order to determine what you can do to it. The key structural guidelines for a deck are: joist spacing and length; beam spans and length; and post size, spacing, and height (see the bottom left drawing). Consult your local code for requirements in your area. The most critical guideline for makeovers is joist spacing (see the chart above). For example, some composite decking products require that joists be spaced closer together than for standard lumber. Identify the joist spacing on your deck and compare with the manufacturer's recommended spacing. If necessary, you can add joists. Note: Whenever you modify the foundation of a deck, make sure to check your local code.

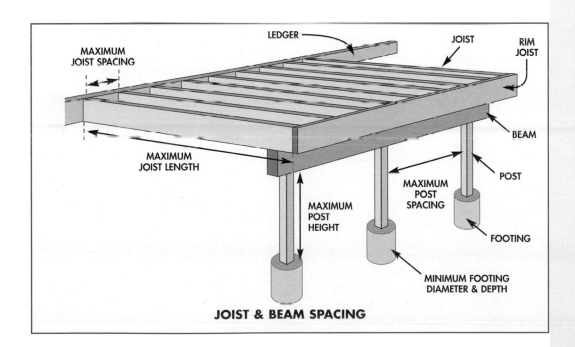

JOIST & BEAM SPACING

- LEDGER
- JOIST
- RIM JOIST
- MAXIMUM JOIST SPACING
- MAXIMUM JOIST LENGTH
- MAXIMUM POST HEIGHT
- MAXIMUM POST SPACING
- BEAM
- POST
- FOOTING
- MINIMUM FOOTING DIAMETER & DEPTH

DECK GUIDELINES,
continued

In addition to the foundation of the deck, there are strict guidelines that must be met for deck railings to protect small children from getting trapped or choked. So if you're planning on installing a new railing, check with your local building inspector to determine railing requirements.

Typically, they'll specify the maximum spacing between the balusters, the maximum space between the bottom rail and the decking, the maximum spacing below a stair rail, and where and when handrails are required (see the drawing above right and the chart below).

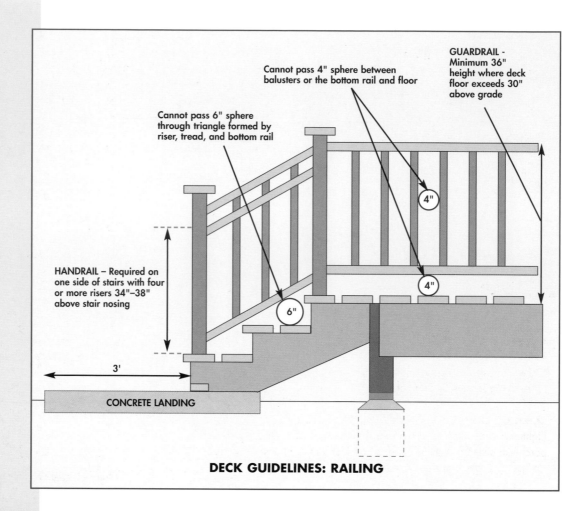

Cannot pass 6" sphere through triangle formed by riser, tread, and bottom rail

Cannot pass 4" sphere between balusters or the bottom rail and floor

GUARDRAIL - Minimum 36" height where deck floor exceeds 30" above grade

HANDRAIL – Required on one side of stairs with four or more risers 34"–38" above stair nosing

3'

CONCRETE LANDING

DECK GUIDELINES: RAILING

CODE REQUIREMENTS FOR RAILINGS

Item Specified	Typical Requirement*
Decks that require railings	All decks 30" or more in height
Stairways that require railings	All stairs having 5 or more steps
Height of railing	36" to 42"; usually 36" for residential and 42" for multi-use or commercial applications.
Space between balusters	4" to 6" maximum
Space between balusters and posts	4" to 6" maximum
Space between bottom rail and deck	2" to 4" maximum

*Consult your local code for actual requirements.

PORCH STYLES

■ Porches are as individual—or uniform—as the houses they grace. Whether a grand pillared entry or a plain concrete stair, a porch serves many functions: It's a resting place for packages, a shelter while you fish for your keys, and a greeting space for visitors. Porches are the introduction to your home: What kind of first impression does yours make?

You may be pleased at the difference a small change can make: Adding a railing, freshening paint, and adding plants can bring charm and personality. For more dramatic change, there's more good news: Today's materials and components permit larger-scale improvements with less cost and maintenance.

Entryway porch. The common entryway porch (made not so common here with the graceful door and pillars) typically offers little more than shelter (above). There may be space for a bench, but the purpose is to serve as the home's entry point.

Open porch. The open porch design below is basically an overhead (lightened with skylights), on a raised surface of cedar. Still, it gives the porch-like benefits of shelter, and a transition into the home. Plantings and pillars add elegance.

Side porch. When the goal is more privacy and quiet, a porch attached to the side of the home works perfectly (above). This side design can also take advantage of a prettier view, or a more sheltered yard area, than the front of the residence might offer.

Dual entry/exit porch. There's plenty of access to this dual entry/exit porch (right), with stairs to and from both the front walk and the side drive. This is a real plus for foot-traffic flow.

Wraparound porch. A classic, from the days when porches were designed for socializing (left). The expansive design provides access to the porch from various rooms within the house, and balances the scale of a larger home.

Three-season porch. Almost a living space, this style porch (right) is enclosed on all sides. It may feature just screens, or more likely storm window inserts, too. In some climates, this can be a four-season porch.

PORCH TYPES

Portico

Full-Width

Wraparound

Side

PORCH TYPES

■ Porches are most often built as an entrance to a house and are usually distinguished from patios by their roofs. The porch roof may be a continuation of the home's roof, or it may be a separate unit. There are four broad types that most porches fit into: portico, full-width, wraparound, and side (see the drawing at left).

Portico. The dictionary defines a portico as a sheltered place often at the entrance to a building. Porticos can vary substantially in width from a simple door-wide shelter that offers only modest protection from the elements, to a structure that's well over half the width of the home. Wider porticos allow for some seating and socializing.

Full-width. The classic front porch is a full-width porch that is as wide as the house. These may be open, partially closed with knee walls, screened in, or enclosed. Most full-width porches have only a single entry point in the front and provide access to the home via a single front door.

Wraparound. When a porch is shaped like an "L" to hug adjacent walls of a home, it's called a wraparound. These porches were designed to provide cool shaded areas for family and friends on hot summer days. Most wraparound porches are open or have knee walls. They may have two or more entry points and often allow access to more than one room in the home.

Side. As towns grew and more and more streets were paved for automobiles, many architects started designing porches for the side of the home. This provided the same cool, shaded spot for relaxing in the summer, but also offered a more private, quieter location away from the noise and traffic of the street.

PORCH GUIDELINES

■ With the exception of the roof, many of the construction details of a porch are similar to those of a deck. Just like a deck, the support system of a porch starts with concrete footings set into the ground. The difference here is that instead of wood posts resting on the foundation to support the floor, many porches replace the posts with a brick pier for a better appearance.

The porch roof can be an extension of the house roof, or it can be a separate section. It is typically supported with large columns of varying size and shape and may or may not be solid. Common guidelines for porches include: roof slope; post size, spacing, and height; and footing size, location, and depth (see the drawing at left). Handrail sizing and location will also be specified; see page 19 for more on this.

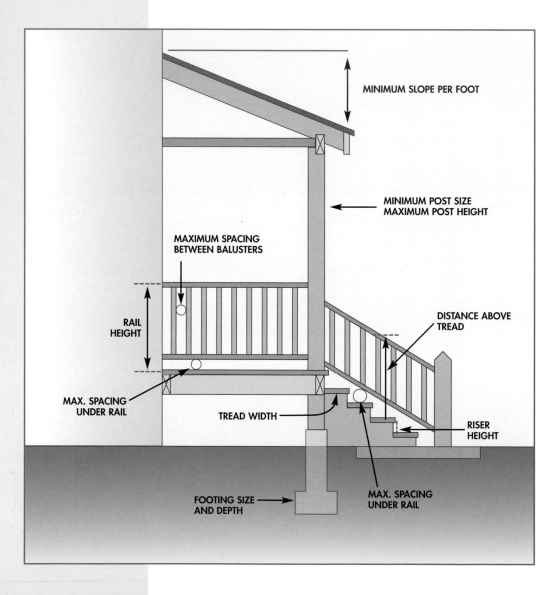

MINIMUM SLOPE PER FOOT

MINIMUM POST SIZE
MAXIMUM POST HEIGHT

MAXIMUM SPACING
BETWEEN BALUSTERS

RAIL
HEIGHT

DISTANCE ABOVE
TREAD

MAX. SPACING
UNDER RAIL

TREAD WIDTH

RISER
HEIGHT

FOOTING SIZE
AND DEPTH

MAX. SPACING
UNDER RAIL

Common porch accessories include steps and a railing system that may or may not use the columns used to support the roof (if applicable); see the drawing below. Since porches are such a highly visible part of a home, great care is usually taken in choosing and installing the railing system. Balusters are often turned or shaped into interesting profiles. The porch may or may not be screened.

The guidelines for porch railings are similar to those for decks to protect small children. You'll need to pay particular attention to spacing between the balusters, spacing beneath the bottom rails, and location and height of the stair handrails. Additionally, since most porches are above ground and have steps or stairs, there are guidelines for number, size, and spacing of stair treads (see the drawing below).

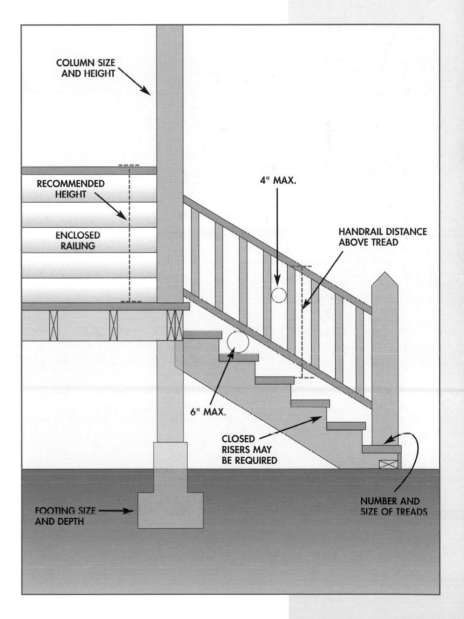

PORCH ORNAMENTATION

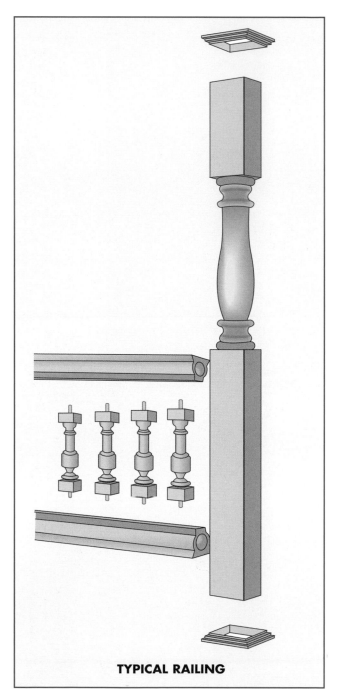

■ Unlike most decks and patios, a porch has a roof that shelters the inner walls and floor from the elements. In addition to keeping you dry and warm/cool, this also creates a kinder environment for building materials, such as the wood columns and handrails or knee walls of the porch. This added protection also lends itself to more decoration in the form of ornamentation that would normally be ravaged by sun, rain, and snow. Porch ornamentation ranges from columns and balusters to the intricately turned or shaped scrollwork common to Victorian homes of yesterday.

Handrails typically span the distance between the porch columns (see the drawing at right). Columns can be plain and simple or turned to delicate profiles. In most cases, the handrail balusters are shaped to match the columns. These usually attach to a top and bottom rail that are affixed to the columns. The columns attach to the porch floor and roof via a set of shaped flanges or base caps.

TYPICAL RAILING

COMMON MOLDINGS

Porch scrollwork or "gingerbread" is a delightful way to add a distinctive touch to your porch. If you're handy with a scroll saw, you can make these pieces yourself—just make sure to use an exterior-rated wood such as cedar or redwood. Premade scrollwork is also available in either wood or urethane foam.

All of the shapes shown in the drawing at left are manufactured by Fypon (www.fypon.com) and are made from easy-to-install foam (see page 112 for more on installing ornamentation). In most cases, installation is simply a matter of finding the ideal location for the scrollwork and attaching it with glue and exterior-rated fasteners.

PATIO STYLES

Whether a simple concrete slab or a tiled poolside retreat, a patio can add special enjoyment and appeal to a home. For many, "the good life" in warm weather means entertaining, playing, and dining outdoors. If your patio isn't keeping up with your life, there's never been a better time to improve your outdoor space.

Maybe a new surface underfoot and more stylish furniture will be all you need. Or, you might invest in tile, pavers, or an arbor to make a bigger splash. Whatever your makeover goals, there are materials and products to help you achieve them without drowning your budget.

Brick-and-sand patio. This is the simplest patio to install. Bricks are laid in the desired pattern (above) on a prepared bed of gravel, and then the spaces between the bricks are filled in with sand.

Pavers patio. Patio pavers are a popular way to create a patio, offering many shapes, sizes, and colors for a variety of designs, as shown in the photo at right. Interlocking concrete pavers are positioned on a bed of pea gravel or concrete.

Covered patio. Covering a patio creates a sheltered haven that you can enjoy in almost any weather. The cover can be a partial roof (as shown in the photo at right) or can extend to protect the entire patio.

Tiled patio. For the ultimate in good looks and durability, a concrete pad can be tiled to create a distinctive patio (above). Whatever your tile choice among the array available, be sure to use an exterior-rated tile such as porcelain.

Concrete patio. A bed of concrete (right photo) is the most stable patio foundation there is. Depending on climate, the concrete may be a simple slab or a slab with footings. Design choices abound: Pick a pattern imprinted on concrete, or one with a top layer of colorful rock, tile, or even glass.

PATIO GUIDELINES

The guidelines for your patio will vary widely depending on your climate. This is particularly true regarding concrete slabs; see the opposite page. The codes are less stringent for other foundations, such as brick-and-sand or concrete pavers, which don't attach to the home. In some parts of the country, a permit is not required to install or modify one of these types of foundations. One area of concern for patios regarding code is an overhead (if any); see the drawing below.

Patio overheads vary from attached roofs to simple freestanding arbors. For roofs, the way the patio roof attaches to the home is critical to prevent leaks. Also, the slope of the patio roof must meet code specifications in order to shed water and support the roof under snow loads (if applicable). Other guidelines for overheads include: type of roofing allowed (for example, some areas do not allow for corrugated plastic roofing); type and size of blocking (if required); size and length of joists; size and length of beam and allowable spans; size and height of posts; and the minimum allowable clearance under the end of the overhead opposite the house; see the drawing at right.

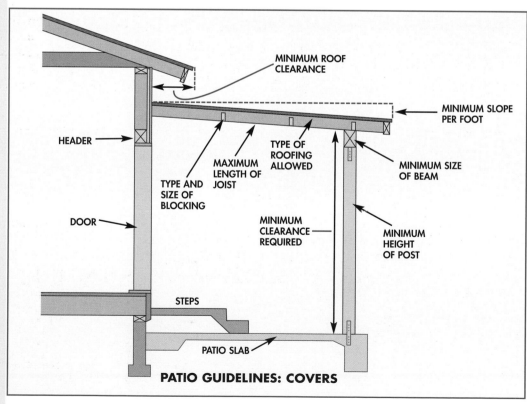

PATIO GUIDELINES: COVERS

HEADER

DOOR

STEPS

PATIO SLAB

TYPE AND SIZE OF BLOCKING

MAXIMUM LENGTH OF JOIST

MINIMUM ROOF CLEARANCE

TYPE OF ROOFING ALLOWED

MINIMUM SLOPE PER FOOT

MINIMUM SIZE OF BEAM

MINIMUM CLEARANCE REQUIRED

MINIMUM HEIGHT OF POST

Guidelines for patio foundations tend to be strict to prevent problems from frost heave. Frost heave occurs when footings in colder climates do not extend below the frost line. When a footing for a concrete pad or slab is above the frost line and the ground freezes, the ground expands and forces the footing (and anything attached to it) to move or "heave." In some cases, it'll only take a few freeze/thaw cycles to loosen hardware, crack foundations, and even break lumber. That's why it's critical that footings be below the frost line. This is also why all inspectors require that footings not be backfilled right after they've been poured, so that the depth of the footing can be checked.

If your makeover calls for a new or replacement slab, make sure to get the work done professionally. At the very least, get a permit and make sure the footings are inspected before proceeding with the makeover. Make sure the footing width and depth and the thickness of the slab all meet or exceed code requirements. Another common patio makeover project is to install new or replacement steps leading from the home out onto the patio. Guidelines for steps include: minimum landing surface, minimum tread width, and maximum riser height; see the drawing at left.

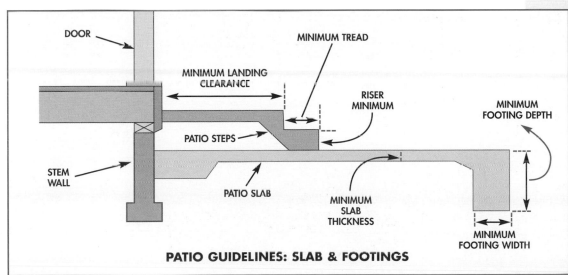

PATIO GUIDELINES: SLAB & FOOTINGS

PAVING PATTERNS

■ Although most concrete patio slabs are not very exciting to look at, they make excellent foundations for a makeover. You can tile over concrete or even cover it with bricks or concrete pavers (see pages 42–43). Both bricks and concrete pavers come in a wide variety of shapes, sizes, and colors.

What this means for you is that there are a world of design possibilities. The most common patterns you can use with bricks are shown in the drawing at right. From the simplest to most complex, they are: stack bond, running bond, basket weave, and herringbone.

Stack bond. The simplest of patterns, stack bond should be used only for small patios. On larger patios it's difficult to keep the bricks aligned. Another use for the stack bond pattern is for framing the perimeter of any of the other patterns.

Running bond. The bricks in the running bond pattern are staggered; this is the easiest to lay down on larger surfaces. This classic pattern looks good in almost any setting, particularly if you use multicolored bricks or tumbled stone.

Basket weave. For greater visual appeal, the basket weave pattern varies the orientation of the bricks. Although complicated-looking, this is still a fairly simple pattern to install.

Herringbone. The interlocking nature of the herringbone pattern makes it one of the more durable patio surfaces, since each brick is held in place by its neighbors. On the flipside, this is a more challenging pattern to lay down and requires much more measuring, layout, and patience to get it right.

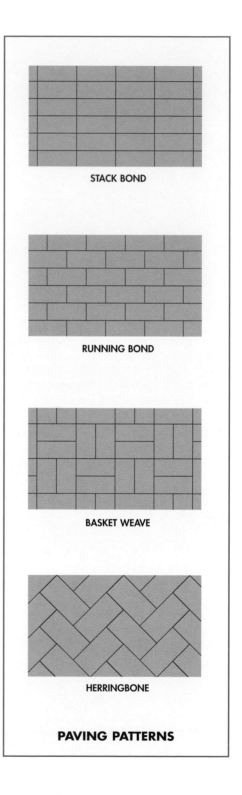

STACK BOND

RUNNING BOND

BASKET WEAVE

HERRINGBONE

PAVING PATTERNS

PATIO ARBORS

If you'd like the added privacy of an overhead for your patio, but don't want to block all the sun, consider adding an arbor (also called a pergola). Arbor styles range from simple covers for patio walkways (like the one shown in the top photo) to complex, full-sized patio covers. Arbors can be free-standing or attached to the home. Freestanding arbors are extremely popular, as they're fairly simple to build and offer plenty of design opportunities.

A typical freestanding arbor is shown in the drawing at left. It consists of a set of vertical posts that support the cross beams. The posts are either set in the ground in concrete piers or are attached to a slab via post anchors. The cross beams are bolted to the posts and support the purlins, which provide some protection from the sun. The size and spacing of the purlins dictates how much sun protection they give. For more on building an arbor, see pages 122–125.

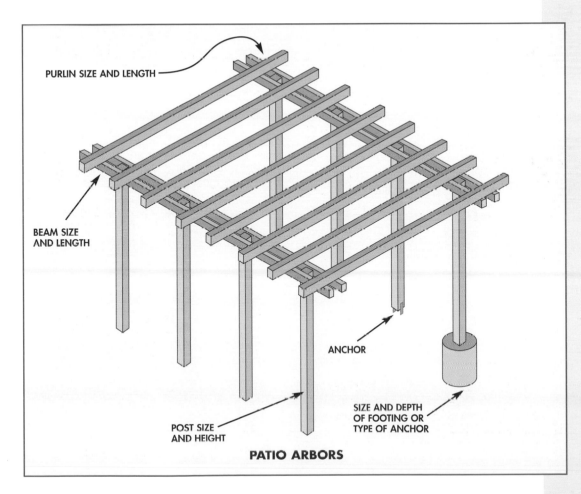

PURLIN SIZE AND LENGTH

BEAM SIZE AND LENGTH

ANCHOR

POST SIZE AND HEIGHT

SIZE AND DEPTH OF FOOTING OR TYPE OF ANCHOR

PATIO ARBORS

2

CHOOSING MATERIALS

Like most aspects of home improvement, the materials available for decks, porches, and patios have multiplied and advanced in the last several years. Wood, of course, remains a classic choice, and there are very specific types and grades of lumber that will serve you well. What's new—or newer? Hardy, handsome composites...vinyl handrail systems... ready-made components...all capable of helping you realize your makeover dreams. With so many options, your outside upgrade can be more do-able than ever before.

But which way should you go? What are the advantages (and possible downsides) of all the materials on the market today? And, how do things like tile, stain, ornamentation, and even windows and doors fit into your picture? You'll be better able to sift through the choices—and answer many of your questions—with the information in this chapter.

LUMBER

There are three exterior-rated woods you can choose from for making over decks and porches: redwood, cedar, and pressure-treated pine.

Redwood. Redwood is both beautiful and durable. Its decay- and insect-resistance and great longevity are legendary. The sapwood of California redwood is nearly white; the heartwood is light red to deep reddish brown (top two pieces in top photo). The grain is straight with a coarse texture. California redwood is light to moderately light and soft. There are over 30 grades of redwood, varying in appearance and durability. For more information on which grade is best for your project, check out the California Redwood Association website at www.calredwood.org.

Western red cedar. Western red cedar is moderately soft and lightweight, is extremely decay-resistant, and exhibits little shrinkage (middle board in top photo). Completely non-resinous, this is one of the most decay-resistant species in America; that's why it's so popular in deck and porch construction. Cedar is also a dimensionally stable wood that lies flat and stays straight. When exposed, it weathers to an attractive silver gray. For more information on Western red cedar, visit the Western Red Cedar Lumber Association website at www.wrcla.org.

Southern pine. Southern pine is the most common wood used in outdoor construction, as it's the least expensive (bottom pieces in top photo). In the past it was treated with a preservative called chromated copper arsenate. Nowadays, a safer alkaline copper quat or copper azole is used. There are two common "grades" of pressure-treated pine: above-ground and ground-contact. Each describes how much preservative is retained by the wood. Ground-contact lumber can touch the soil, or be buried in the ground. For more information on Southern pine, visit the Southern Pine Council website at www.southernpine.com.

COMPOSITE DECK MATERIALS

■ Although composite decking has been around for years, it's finally starting to show up consistently in lumberyards and home centers across the country.

Solid composite materials. Composite materials are made from recycled plastic and ground-up wood fibers with the intent of offering the best of both materials (see the photo at right). Since part of the composition is wood fibers, the decking will weather gray over time; since the wood fibers are small, there is no risk of splinters. The benefit of adding plastic is that the deck boards are much more stable—no warp, and no splitting. Trex, Choice-Dek, Tek-Dek, TimberTech, and Nexwood are all popular choices.

Extruded composite decking. Unlike the solid composites described above, some manufacturers make extruded deck boards. An example of this is TimberTech planking, as shown in the middle photo. This planking is extruded in the form of a tongue-and-groove plank. An extrusion like this is expensive (typically around $5 per square foot), but it offers a number of excellent advantages. First, as with any tongue-and-groove product, the fasteners are hidden—there are no nail "pops" or protruding screws to catch bare feet. Second, by engineering support "braces" into the planks, the end result is a dimensionally stable and lightweight deck board that will stand up extremely well over time (visit the TimberTech website at www.timbertech.com for additional information).

Composite accessories. In addition to deck boards, some manufacturers make composite accessories to match their decking, like the railing system manufactured by TimberTech shown in the bottom photo. These offer the same properties as the decking: no finish required—and no maintenance needed.

VINYL DECK MATERIALS

■ If you've had enough of cleaning, staining, or painting your wood deck, consider replacing the old deck boards with new vinyl decking, or covering them with vinyl deck covers.

Vinyl decking. A number of plastics manufacturers now make vinyl decking. This is typically an extrusion that's designed to replace existing deck boards (see the middle photo). To conceal the open ends of the extrusions, vinyl trim is available. Besides offering the advantage of no maintenance, vinyl decking typically has a ridged top that promotes water runoff and creates a no-slip surface.

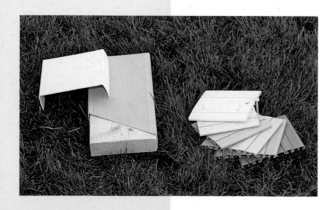

Vinyl deck covers. An alternative to tearing up and replacing worn-out deck boards is to cover your old decking with a vinyl deck "cap" developed by Durable Deck. This system can be installed directly over an existing deck—even over concrete (see the bottom photo). The only requirement is that the old surface be structurally sound. There are two types of cap: One is a hollow shell that snaps in place over a standard 2×6 deck board. The other system is a thin vinyl extrusion that's screwed directly to the old decking; then the screws are concealed with a snap-in vinyl strip. (For more on installing this type of system, see pages 92–95.) For more information on Durable Deck, visit their website at www.durabledeck.com.

OUTDOOR FASTENERS

■ Anytime you fasten together parts with screws or nails as part of an exterior makeover, make sure they're rated for exterior use. As a general rule of thumb, screws will always hold better than nails and will have less tendency to loosen over time (as nails are prone to). Exterior-rated screws, from left to right in the top photo, are: galvanized, coated (two types), stainless steel, silicon-bronze, and brass. Exterior-rated nails, from left to right in the middle photo, are aluminum, stainless steel, and galvanized.

Galvanized. The standard in material for outdoor screws and nails is steel, which is then galvanized to seal against moisture. Whenever possible, specify hot-dipped galvanized fasteners for your projects, as these hold up the best over time.

Coated. A relative newcomer to the fastener market, vinyl-coated screws come in two colors, tan and green, and are touted as weather-resistant. The screws are coated with a thin layer of vinyl that seals the metal. This works great as long as the coating isn't disturbed. The problem is that when you drive the screw through a piece of wood, the coating rubs off. An improved variation on this theme is the composite decking TrapEase screws manufactured by

FastenMaster (third screw from the left in the top photo). These screws are covered with a proprietary coating that combines zinc and epoxy. Additionally, these screws have two sets of threads: one to pull the fastener into the floor joists, and another to pull the decking down tight against the joists.

Stainless steel. We prefer stainless steel fasteners for our makeover projects because their tougher coating doesn't wear off and they hold up the best over time. Note that this kind of durability comes at a price: Stainless steel fasteners typically cost twice as much as galvanized. Stainless steel screws can be found at some hardware stores and home centers or at www.mcfeelys.com.

Bronze. Bronze screws have been popular in the boatbuilding trade for years, as they stand up extremely well to the elements. When they're first made, they have the color of a fresh penny, but they will oxidize and darken over time. This darker color makes silicon-bronze an excellent choice for a Western cedar or redwood deck, as the screws will blend right in as the deck ages.

Brass. Brass screws have also been used in the boatbuilding business, but find less use in deck and porch construction because the metal is so soft. It tends to strip and/or break easily. If you do use brass screws, you can reduce the risk of damage by drilling appropriate-sized pilot holes.

HIDDEN DECKING FASTENERS

Regardless of what type of fastener you use to secure a deck board to the floor joists, you're still left with an exposed fastener that will eventually succumb to the elements and deteriorate. This usually leads to corrosion and staining. One way to eliminate this problem is to use a hidden fastening system. This way, the fasteners won't be exposed and can't stain your deck boards—and you'll be left with a much cleaner-looking deck surface. There are four common hidden deck-fastening systems. From top to bottom in the drawing they are: Deckmaster, Shadoe® Track, deck board ties, and the EB•TY system.

Deckmaster. The Deckmaster hidden system is a special metal bracket that attaches to the joists and provides a method for attaching the deck boards from underneath, leaving no fasteners exposed. The system shown here is manufactured by Grabber under the brand name Deckmaster (www.deckmaster.com). The brackets are available either galvanized or in stainless steel. This system works extremely well for raised decks with clearance below. On a low-lying deck with little or no clearance, you'll need to use a right-angle drill to drive in the screws.

Shadoe Track. A hidden deck fastening that's similar to Deckmaster is Shadoe Track (www.shadoetrack.com). This system also utilizes a bracket to secure the deck boards. It's different in that it attaches to the top of the floor joists instead of the side, as with the Deckmaster system.

Deck board ties. Deck board ties are another way to attach deck boards without leaving fasteners exposed. The deck board ties shown here are manufactured by Simpson Strong-Tie (www.strongtie.com) and each is installed with a single 10d nail. Locator prongs help position the clip for easier installation. Note that with all hidden fastening systems it's imperative to check your local building code to make sure they are allowed in your area.

EB•TY. A unique hidden fastening system developed by Swan Secure Products (www.swansecure.com) is the EB•TY fastening system. The heart of the system is a plastic, football-shaped "biscuit" that fits into slots cut in the deck boards with a biscuit joiner.

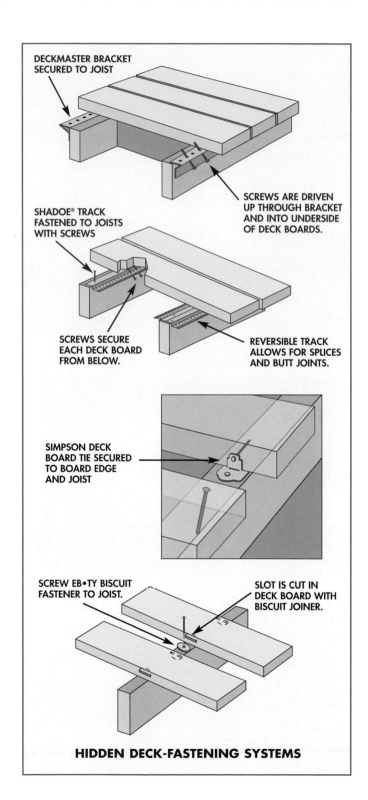

DECKMASTER BRACKET SECURED TO JOIST

SCREWS ARE DRIVEN UP THROUGH BRACKET AND INTO UNDERSIDE OF DECK BOARDS.

SHADOE® TRACK FASTENED TO JOISTS WITH SCREWS

SCREWS SECURE EACH DECK BOARD FROM BELOW.

REVERSIBLE TRACK ALLOWS FOR SPLICES AND BUTT JOINTS.

SIMPSON DECK BOARD TIE SECURED TO BOARD EDGE AND JOIST

SCREW EB•TY BISCUIT FASTENER TO JOIST.

SLOT IS CUT IN DECK BOARD WITH BISCUIT JOINER.

HIDDEN DECK-FASTENING SYSTEMS

FRAMING CONNECTORS

Metal framing connectors are designed for use on 2-by projects where you need to quickly attach parts together. The toughness of metal adds considerable rigidity and strength to any project. Framing connectors that you'll find handy for your makeover projects include: post caps, post bases, fence brackets, joist hangers, staircase angles, and reinforcing angles (see the drawing below).

Post caps. A post cap makes the transition from one framing member to another—quite often from post to beam. A pair of adjustable post caps can be spaced apart to fit a wide variety of framing situations. Retrofit post caps are also installed in pairs and are suitable for heavier loads than adjustable base caps.

Post bases. Post bases may be adjustable or nonadjustable. The adjustable type offers moisture protection by lifting the post off the footing. This space also creates clearance for the washer and nut used to secure the post base to a footing via a J-bolt. A slot in the bottom of the base allows you to slide it back and forth to fine-tune its position. The nonadjustable base offers quick installation: You insert its prongs into the wet footing. The disadvantage here is that once the concrete sets up, you can't adjust its position.

Fence brackets. One of the quickest ways to secure a deck, porch, or patio railing to a column is to use a fence bracket. These brackets are attached to the column, and then the rail is fitted into the bracket and secured.

Joist Hangers. Joist hangers are by far the most often-used framing connectors for decks and porches. They're designed to support a joist, girder, or other framing member from a post, beam, rim joist, header, etc. Joist hangers create a much stronger joint than is possible by simply nailing framing members together. Safety Note: In order for joist hangers to be able to reliably support their designated load, they must be installed with special fasteners called joist hanger nails.

Staircase Angles. Staircase angles are a quick way to build a structurally sound staircase. They attach to the stringer or carriage with joist hanger nails and support the treads.

Reinforcing angles. Many local building codes require reinforcing angles in numerous situations, such as where floor joists meet headers or rim joists, and where studs meet sole plates. Check with your local building inspector to identify what type of reinforcement (if any) is required in your area.

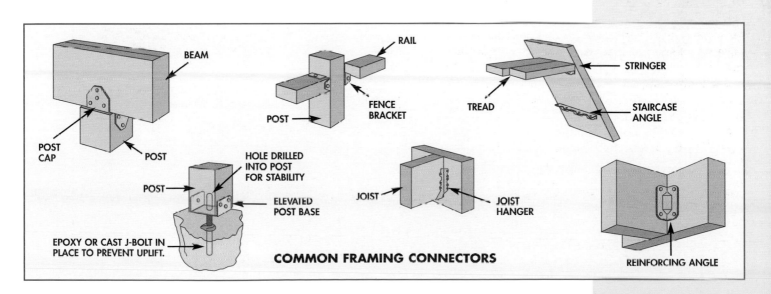

COMMON FRAMING CONNECTORS

READY-MADE DECK PARTS

■ There are many ready-made parts that make upgrading a deck easy. They include: handrail systems, post caps, and seating brackets.

Handrail systems. Of all the ready-made parts available for a deck project, handrail systems come in the widest variety of shapes and sizes. That's because manufacturers realize that every homeowner wants their deck to be unique. With this in mind, you'll find square balusters and turned spindles in a variety of profiles and materials—most commonly pressure-treated pine and cedar. As with balusters, you'll find posts in both pressure-treated pine and cedar, but with many fewer profile options; most home centers carry just one or two designs. Alternatively, many home centers now carry handrail systems made from composites and vinyl, like the one shown in the drawing at right.

Decorative caps. You can spice up a plain post by adding one of the many decorative caps available. Caps can be square cut, shaped, or turned from pressure-treated pine or cedar. Other varieties include pressed metal caps and caps that combine metal and wood, and composite or vinyl caps. Finally, ingenious lighting manufacturers combine a low-voltage light with a decorative metal or vinyl fixture to provide both a visually interesting cap and lighting for the deck.

Seating brackets. If your makeover plans call for adding seating to your deck, consider purchasing one of the many different types of premade seating brackets available. These metal brackets vary in type and style and may be flat or tubular in construction. Most are designed to accept deck lumber for the seat and back, as shown in the drawing at right.

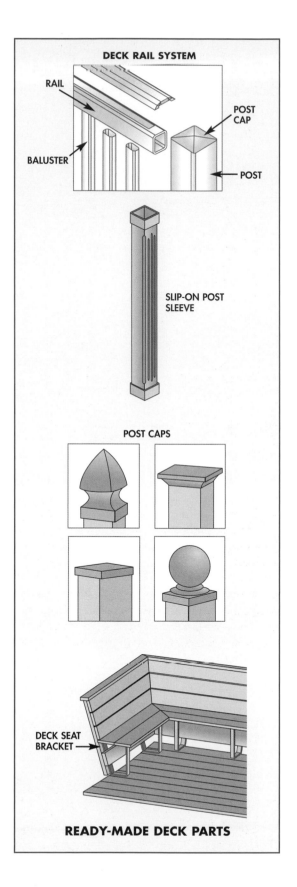

READY-MADE DECK PARTS

PORCH MATERIALS

■ When a porch is your makeover target, there are three broad groups of materials you may be using: siding, wainscoting, and flooring.

Siding. Although the odds are you won't be replacing siding for a porch makeover, you may need some if you're adding knee walls to the porch. In this case, you'll want to match your existing siding. There are two types of commonly available siding: tongue-and-groove siding (top pieces in photo above right) and hardboard siding

(bottom pieces in photo above right). Tongue-and-groove siding is usually milled from cedar and can be stained or painted. Hardboard siding comes prefinished in a variety of colors. (Although most home centers stock only one or two colors, they can special-order siding to match your home.)

Wainscoting. On some porches, the interior knee walls and the porch ceiling are often wainscoting. Wainscoting is thin, tongue-and-grooved planks that slip together easily and create a distinctive surface— the surface on most wainscoting is beaded like the planks shown in the middle photo. Wainscoting is available in a number of wood species—finished or unfinished—or in a prefinished engineered wood like medium-density fiberboard, called MDF.

Flooring. If you need to replace or repair part of a porch floor as part of your makeover, you'll most likely want to use pressure-treated tongue-and-groove flooring like that shown in the bottom photo. You can order this at most home centers. For more on porch flooring, visit the Southern Pine Council website at www.southernpine.com.

READY-MADE PORCH PARTS

■ As with decks, you can find various pre-made parts to speed along your porch makeover. These include columns, handrail systems, and ornamentation (see page 40 for more on ornamentation).

Porch columns. When you look for new columns to make over your porch, it's important to know that there are two basic types available: structural and nonstructural. Structural columns are designed to bear the load of the porch roof. Their size, length, and position are defined by your local codes. Replacing structural columns is a job best left to a pro. Nonstructural columns are purely decorative. These are designed to wrap around or cover an existing column—typically a boring, square 4×4 or a round metal pole. Structural columns are usually made of wood, while nonstructural can be made of urethane foam or plastic. You may find one or two nonstructural columns at your local home center, but don't be satisfied with this limited selection. A huge variety of columns is available. Two websites to visit for column choices are www.fypon.com and www.outwater.com.

Handrail systems. You'll find that most manufacturers of porch columns also make handrail systems to match. Some of these systems are of wood, but many are urethane foam or plastic. What's really nice about most of these systems is that the rails are pre-drilled for the balusters, so assembly is a snap. If you do decide to go with a wood system, look for parts that are pre-finished or pre-primed to make final painting easier.

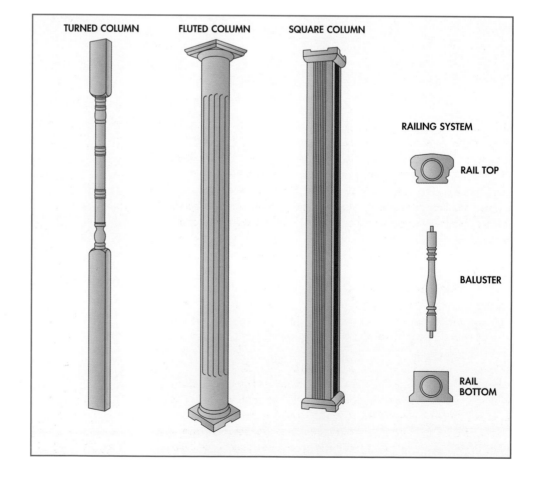

TURNED COLUMN FLUTED COLUMN SQUARE COLUMN

RAILING SYSTEM

RAIL TOP

BALUSTER

RAIL BOTTOM

WINDOWS AND DOORS

■ If replacing a window or door is part of your makeover, you'll want to educate yourself about the various options available. Take your window or door measurements to a local home center and browse through the product catalogs to see what's available. Unless you're replacing a stock size, they'll most likely have to order a replacement.

Windows. If you're replacing a window that looks out onto a deck, porch, or patio, consider replacing it with one of the three specialty types discussed here: bay, bow, or decorative. A bay window protrudes out from an exterior wall to make a room feel larger without the need for expensive structural changes. They are typically made up of three or more windows that project out from the house at 30, 45, or 90 degrees. The center section is usually parallel with the exterior wall and is made up of one or two units. Since bay window units are heavy, care must be taken to support the unit during and after installation.

Bow windows are often confused with bay windows, as they appear somewhat similar. The main difference between the two is that a bow window typically has four or five sections that are formed into a graceful curve or bow. Choosing between a bay and a bow window is really a matter of aesthetics: Which do you think will look better on the exterior of the house—the angular look of a bay window or the flowing curve of a bow window? The variety of decorative window styles, shapes, and sizes on the market is staggering. Common shapes are: octagon, triangle, trapezoid, pentagon with a flat top, pentagon, hexagon with a flat top, quarter circle, half circle, oval, half ellipse, half cloverleaf, gothic arch, arch top, and full circle—just to name a few. Because of their unique shape, most decorative windows are fixed, though some are operating (able to be opened).

Doors. Shopping for a new front door can be daunting: There are so many materials, styles, and features to choose from. Start by deciding what type of door material will work best for you. Two common choices are solid wood and metal. Solid-wood doors offer natural beauty and can be stained or painted to fit your décor. Metal doors can also be painted and they offer stability, strength, and good insulating properties. If you're planning on painting the door, consider a metal door; for a natural look, go with solid wood (or check out the new metal doors that have an outer skin of wood veneer). For more on replacing a door, see pages 158–161.

The sliding door has become the door of choice for many homeowners who have a deck. Its large glass sections provide unrestricted viewing, and one or both of the panels slide open to provide ventilation as well as easy access to a deck or porch. The frames and panels of sliding doors can be made of solid wood, aluminum, or vinyl. In most cases, only one of the panels slides; more expensive sliding doors are available where both panels slide. Swinging doors are basically a pair of standard doors built into a single jamb. One door is hinged for left-handed operation and the other door is hinged for right-handed. Many homeowners choose swinging doors over sliding doors for access to their patio or deck because both doors swing open for maximum ventilation.

ORNAMENTATION

When you want a distinctive touch for your porch, consider adding some ornamentation. Ornamentation options vary from simple brackets to complex turned or scrolled panels, like those underneath the porch roof in the top photo. Regardless of the look you're after, you'll find that there are three main materials used for ornamentation: wood, plastic, and urethane foam.

Wood. In years past, all fancy ornamentation for homes—particularly Victorians—was made of wood. The intricate patterns were usually cut by hand with a coping saw or, as technology progressed, with a power saber saw or scroll saw. Because this was manually intensive, scrollwork like this tended to be expensive. But cutting intricate patterns in wood creates some problems. First, the numerous cutouts often left portions of the scrollwork very fragile. Additionally, the cutouts made it difficult to paint—which you had to do to protect the wood from the elements. Finally, since wood expands and contracts as the seasons change, wood scrollwork had a tendency to work itself loose over time. All of this meant that constant maintenance was required.

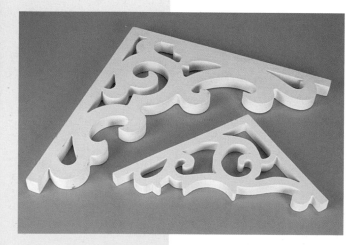

Plastic. As the plastics industry evolved, more and more wood parts were replaced with vinyl. Eventually, forms were designed to create intricate scrollwork. Because the scrollwork was made on a machine and not by hand, it was a lot cheaper. The problem with most plastic scrollwork is that it doesn't take paint very well and tends to crack and peel when exposed to the elements. If all you want is white, plastic scrollwork may work for you; just keep in mind that almost all white plastic will yellow with age.

Urethane foam. Fortunately for fans of ornamentation, urethane foam eventually came to the rescue. This type of scrollwork is lightweight, takes paint well, won't move with seasonal changes, and is easy to install. The scrollwork comes pre-primed so you can paint it any color you want—just make sure to use a quality exterior paint. The brackets shown in the photo at left are just two of dozens of sizes and shapes available from Fypon. Visit their website at www.fypon.com to browse through their choices.

ROOFING MATERIALS

Roofing materials vary widely in appearance, durability, and ease of installation. Porch roofs lend themselves to asphalt shingles to match the existing roof, while decks and patios often use corrugated roofing.

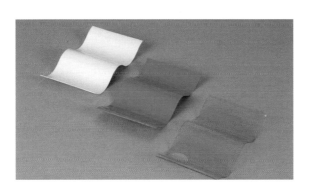

Asphalt shingles. Asphalt shingles are the most common roofing material because they are inexpensive, are easy to install, and last 15 to 20 years. They are available in a wide variety of colors and styles, the most popular styles being architectural, random-tab, and three-tab strips. They are suitable for every climate but should be used only on roofs with a minimum of a 4-in-12 slope. Wood shingles and shakes are lighter than asphalt shingles, weigh less, and better withstand the freeze/thaw cycles common in cold climates. On the downside, they're expensive and time-consuming to install.

Corrugated roofing. Plastic corrugated roofing is an excellent choice for deck and patio overheads. Plastic roofing like this used to be difficult to install. Now, though, most manufacturers have developed homeowner-friendly systems that snap together, so installation is a breeze. Corrugated roofing is commonly available in white, green, and clear plastic, as shown in the middle photo. (Visit the Palram Americas website at www.suntuf.com for more on corrugated roofing materials.) Since all roofing expands and contracts with heat and cold, special flexible fasteners must be used to keep the fastener holes sealed. For more on installing a corrugated roof, see pages 116–121.

PATIO MATERIALS

■ Patios can be made using brick or concrete pavers or poured concrete. Pouring concrete is a job best left to professionals. But if you want to cover an existing slab with bricks or pavers, or you want to make a new patio with brick or concrete pavers, you'll need to know how they differ and their advantages and disadvantages. Bricks and concrete pavers that are set into a sand base (sometimes called sand-set) are easy to maintain: All you have to do is lift out a cracked or unlevel brick and either replace it or add or subtract sand from underneath. And, because they're not permanently bonded to their base, there's little chance of cracking.

Bricks. Standard paving bricks are made from a mixture of shale and clay and measure 3⅝" wide by 7⅝" long or 4" wide by 8" long. You'll find varying thicknesses and colors, as shown in the photo above. When used on a sand bed, these bricks are fitted closely together and any gaps between them are filled with sand. If you live in a climate where the ground freezes, make sure to purchase bricks that are SX-rated, as these can stand up to freezing temperatures without cracking.

There are two common types of bricks available: common brick and face brick. Common brick has a rough texture, and face brick has a slick surface. Common brick is less expensive than face brick and its non-glare surface creates excellent traction. It has a porous surface that readily absorbs moisture (and, unfortunately, food spills, which can be difficult to remove). In freezing climates, this porosity can also lead to breakage when a moist brick freezes during daily freeze/thaw cycles. Face brick is very attractive but should be used only in areas where safety is not a concern, such as edgings, and on raised beds, where there will be no foot traffic.

Pavers. Molded pavers are made of cast concrete or fired brick (bottom left photo). They are generally much denser than standard bricks and are therefore much more difficult to cut. With this in mind, it's best if you plan the design to minimize cutting. If you do need concrete pavers cut, most home centers and brick-yards will do this for you for a small fee.

You'll find a sizable range of interlocking pavers at most home and garden centers. The interlocking nature of their design helps to create a stable patio because they have less tendency to shift position after they're installed. A standard brick paver makes an excellent border for these interlocking pavers.

Edging. In addition to bricks and pavers, you'll also find a variety of edging available at most home and garden centers, as shown in the photo at right. A popular style for borders and for landscaping  are the scalloped-edged pieces—either curved or flat. These are most often cast from porous brick material. If you're looking for something more durable, choose one of the many precast concrete edging pieces. Like concrete pavers, most of these offer an interlocking design that makes them easy to install and less prone to shifting once in place.

Tile. Tile can be a great way to improve the look of a concrete slab—as long as you choose the appropriate tile (below right). Because this tile will be exposed to the elements, it's important to choose both tile and grout that are rated for exterior use. Most ceramic tile is unsuitable for outdoor use. Instead, choose porcelain tile. Although it's harder to cut, it'll stand up better over time. If you have any questions, contact a reputable tile contractor or showroom in your area.

STAIN, PAINT, AND SEALERS

■ After all the hard work of making over a deck, porch, or patio, you'll want to protect newly installed surfaces with stain, paint, or sealers. If you're protecting wood, the type of finish you choose will depend on how much wood grain you want to see and what kind of protection you're after.

How often you need to reapply a finish to wood parts depends on its existing finish and the local weather conditions. Decks exposed to extreme climates (such as the cold winters of Minnesota or the hot summers of Arizona) require more attention than a deck in a mild region.

Likewise, the type of finish you use will affect the frequency of maintenance. Transparent water sealants often need to be refreshed every year; solid-color stains may need less frequent attention. Note that although most composite decking doesn't require a finish, many of them will accept one—just realize that once you apply one, the finish will need regular attention.

Stain and clear topcoats. To see the most wood grain, use a clear wood finish. An exterior-rated polyurethane or a marine "spar" varnish are both good choices. But realize that these will most likely need annual attention in the form of touch-up work. Select a clear topcoat with UV blockers to protect the wood from the sun. For less visible grain, choose a semi-transparent stain. To hide the grain, use a solid-color stain. You'll find a huge assortment of colors available at most home centers and hardware stores, as shown in the top photo.

Paint. Do you want to completely obscure the underlying wood or get it to match or accent your existing trim or house color? Paint is an obvious choice. As with stain, you'll find a wide variety of colors available, as shown in the middle photo. Pick an exterior-grade paint. Although the latex paints are easier to clean up, we've found that the oil-based exterior paints hold up better over time.

Deck cleaners. There are a number of chemical products available (often referred to as deck cleaners, brighteners, or deck wash) that can make quick work of renewing tired-looking deck boards, as shown in the bottom photo. All of these products typically contain a mild acid, either sodium hypochlorite or oxalic acid, that dissolves dirt and grime and chemically lightens the wood. Most can be sprayed on and will do their work without needing scrubbing: Simply wait 10 to 15 minutes, hose down the deck, and it will look as good as new (for more on deck cleaning, see pages 86–87).

Deck sealers. One of the most popular finishes used to protect a wood deck is a transparent water sealer like the type shown in the top photo. Water sealers are penetrating oil formulas that soak down into porous materials and create a moisture barrier that still lets the wood breathe. Most sealers dry clear and allow the wood to weather naturally. Water sealers are easy to apply with an ordinary garden sprayer and can be "refreshed" with periodic applications (if you see dark stain on your deck after it rains, it's time for another coat).

FINISHING CONCRETE

■ Often, all a concrete patio or porch floor needs to have a fresh look is a thorough cleaning followed by the application of a concrete stain or paint.

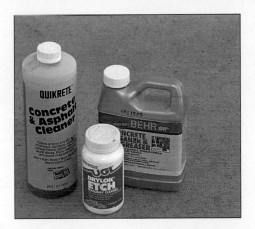

Cleaners. There are a number of concrete cleaners on the market that do an excellent job of removing dirt and stains from concrete. They're available in dry or liquid concentrate form that you mix with water, as shown in the photo at left. The liquid concentrates tend to mix quicker. Follow the instructions carefully and protect yourself by wearing old clothes and eye protection. For more on cleaning concrete, see page 138.

Stain. Many homeowners don't realize that you can stain concrete, but it's easy to do. Stains are an excellent way to impart color to concrete without worrying about the regular maintenance that paint usually needs. Most stains are semi-transparent, so you'll still be able to see that the underlying surface is concrete, as shown in the photo above. These are easy to apply with a roller and can be refreshed as needed by first cleaning the concrete and then applying a fresh coat of stain.

Paint. One of the best ways to seal concrete and keep out dirt and debris is to paint it. Most paint manufacturers sell paint designed specifically for covering concrete, as shown in the photo above. Because the paint bonds to the concrete itself, it's imperative that the concrete be super clean and completely dry before applying the paint. See pages 140–141 for more on painting concrete.

3

OUTDOOR SYSTEMS

Underneath the paint or stain...in back of the stairs... above, in the roof overhang...these are the places where "systems" rule. A revamp of a deck, porch, or patio often involves adding or subtracting structural elements like porch columns, handrails, or even windows and doors. Before you attempt any of these projects, it's important for you to understand the whole picture—that is, how the separate parts, or systems, of a deck, porch, or patio all work together.

Defining and explaining these systems is what this chapter is about. We'll cover everything from deck, porch, and patio anatomy to foundations and roofing. You may not need to know it all, but in these cases, a little knowledge is a powerful thing. Note: Building codes vary greatly from town to town and state to state. Make sure to check with your local building inspection office before modifying a deck, porch, or patio. And remember, your safety is their primary concern.

DECK ANATOMY

Regardless of the type of deck you're making over, it's important to have a basic understanding of deck construction, including the common parts and terms, in order to determine what you can or cannot do to the deck. No matter how simple or complex a deck is, every deck can be broken down into three main parts: the support system, the foundation, and the decking.

The support system. A deck is supported by either ledgers or footings, or both. In most cases a ledger attaches to the house to support one-half the deck weight, and the other half is supported by concrete footings. The weight of the deck is transferred to the footings by way of posts and beams. In the drawing below, the posts run vertically between the concrete footings and a long horizontal support beam, which is often built up from 2-by stock. The beam can be located directly under the end of the foundation, or the foundation can extend past the beam to create a cantilevered deck as shown. The beam can rest directly on top of the posts, or be bolted to the sides of them.

The foundation. In its simplest form, the foundation for a deck is an open frame similar to a framed wall that's lying on its side. The structural member that attaches the frame to the home is the ledger. The joists that create the perimeter of the frame are called rim joists; these are commonly covered with decorative trim boards known as fascia. The joists inside the frame that connect the ledger to the opposite rim joist are called field joists. The field joists typically attach to the ledger by way of joist hangers and are screwed to the rim joist or supported with joist hangers.

The decking. The most visible part of the deck, the decking or deck boards, goes on last. In most cases, the boards run parallel to the house and attach directly to the foundation. Depending on the visual effect desired, you can install a wide variety of patterns. Although deck boards made of wood are still the most common type used, consider one of the alternatives available (see page 31). These new materials offer flat, stable decking that won't warp and require little maintenance.

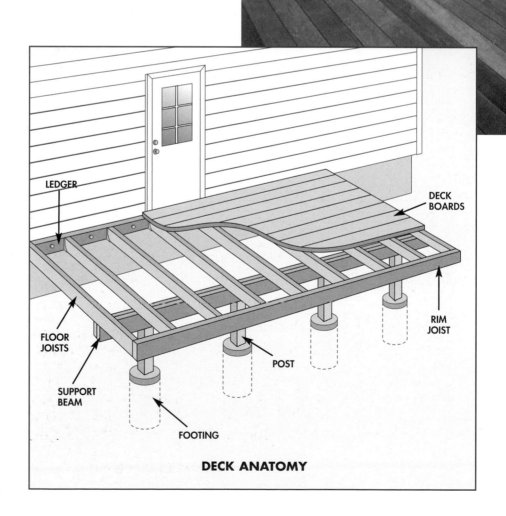

LEDGER

DECK BOARDS

FLOOR JOISTS

SUPPORT BEAM

FOOTING

POST

RIM JOIST

DECK ANATOMY

DECK FOUNDATIONS

Unlike patios, which are installed directly on the ground, decks are usually built above ground for a couple of reasons. First, most homes require steps up for access, and raising a deck to the door threshold provides a seamless transition. Second, the foundations of decks are built of wood (usually pressure-treated). Although the wood is designed to stand up to the elements, it will last longer if kept clean and mostly dry. Raising it above ground accomplishes both. Deck support is provided by either ledgers or footings.

The other half of a deck's weight (or the full weight, if the deck is freestanding) is borne by the footings, as shown in the drawing below. Footings are usually concrete columns set into the ground to distribute the load of the deck. The diameter and depth of the footings depends on the weight of the deck and the climate. For the average deck, an 8" to 10" diameter works well. In order for the footing to remain stable in all weather conditions, it must go well below the frost line (the local building inspector can tell you how far down to dig). Concrete can be poured directly into a hole or into a form. In temperate climates, precast piers can be installed on top of shallow concrete pads.

The simplest way to create a footing is to dig a hole, pour in cement, and either embed a post (as shown) or install post base caps. The disadvantage to this method is that it tends to use a lot more concrete than is necessary to fill the hole. The advantage: You don't have to backfill, and if you make the base bell-shaped (as shown), it will firmly anchor the footing in the ground. Although footings that use a form require a bit more work those without, there are advantages. The biggest is that the form accurately defines how much concrete you'll need. Most home centers have a chart that will tell you exactly how many bags of ready-mix concrete you'll need to fill a form, regardless of its depth or diameter. The disadvantage is that you have to cut and position the form, as well as backfill after the concrete sets.

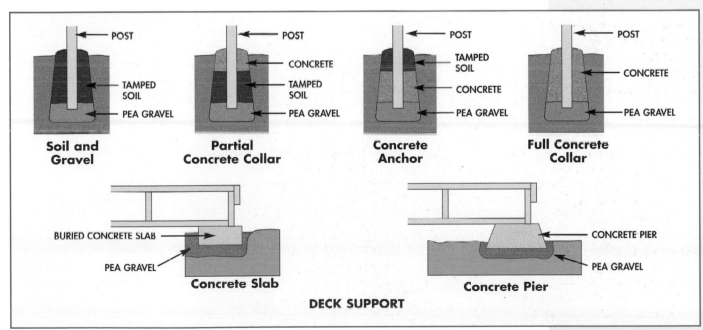

DECK SUPPORT

DECK LEDGERS

A ledger is basically a stout plank of lumber that's attached directly to the house to support one end of the deck (see the drawing at right). The size of the ledger depends on the weight of the deck and how it's attached to the house. How it attaches depends primarily on the home's exterior (siding, stucco, or brick). Common methods include securing it with lag screws and bolting it to the rim joists.

Since a ledger must support one-half the deck weight, it absolutely must be installed properly. Horror stories of decks shearing off the sides of homes and collapsing are usually due to improper ledger installation. The best method is to bolt the ledger to the rim joist of the house, as shown. To prevent moisture problems, flashing is installed above the ledger and washers are inserted between the ledger and the house to allow for drainage.

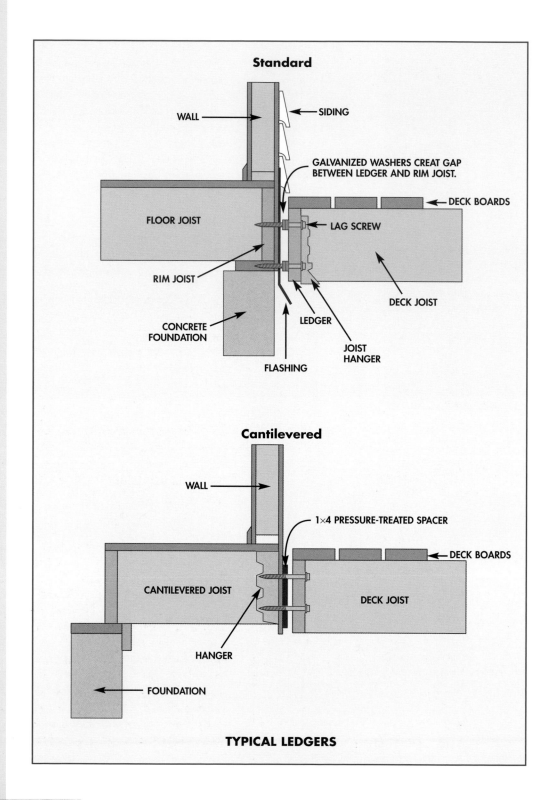

Standard

WALL — SIDING

GALVANIZED WASHERS CREAT GAP BETWEEN LEDGER AND RIM JOIST.

DECK BOARDS

FLOOR JOIST — LAG SCREW

RIM JOIST — DECK JOIST

CONCRETE FOUNDATION — LEDGER

JOIST HANGER

FLASHING

Cantilevered

WALL

1×4 PRESSURE-TREATED SPACER

DECK BOARDS

CANTILEVERED JOIST — DECK JOIST

HANGER

FOUNDATION

TYPICAL LEDGERS

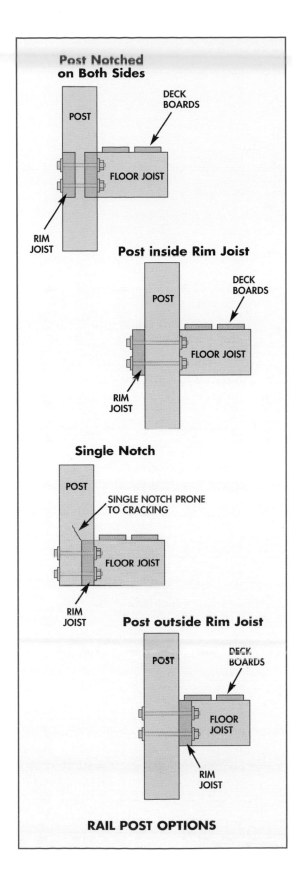

Post Notched on Both Sides

POST

DECK BOARDS

FLOOR JOIST

RIM JOIST

Post inside Rim Joist

POST

DECK BOARDS

FLOOR JOIST

RIM JOIST

Single Notch

POST

SINGLE NOTCH PRONE TO CRACKING

FLOOR JOIST

RIM JOIST

Post outside Rim Joist

POST

DECK BOARDS

FLOOR JOIST

RIM JOIST

RAIL POST OPTIONS

POST OPTIONS

■ The foundation of a sturdy handrail system is the posts to which rails and balusters attach. There are three common ways of attaching posts to the foundation of the deck: outside the rim joists, inside the rim joists, and continuous posts. Each of these methods has pros and cons.

Posts on outside of joists. The simplest way to attach railing posts to a deck is to bolt them to the outside face of the rim joists (see the drawing at left). This method looks fine from the deck side, but doesn't project the neatest appearance from the deck's exterior. There are, however, a couple of ways to camouflage the posts. One way is to cut notches on the bottom ends so the post fits over the rim joists. Although this does create a slimmer profile, it does weaken the post. Another option is to miter the bottom ends for a cleaner look.

Posts on inside of joists. A less conspicuous but more labor-intensive way to attach deck railing posts is to bolt them to the inside face of the rim joists (see the drawing at left). This method takes advance planning since the posts need to be installed before the decking is laid down. The extra labor involved is twofold. First, you'll need to countersink the bolt holes in the rim joists so that the fascia will lie flat when it's installed. Second, you'll have to notch and fit the deck boards around the posts. On the plus side, this method provides the cleanest appearance.

Continuous posts. A third method for installing posts for a deck rail is to extend the posts that support the beam and connect to footings up high enough that they can serve as a railing. Although this is one of the sturdiest ways to install a post, not only does it require the most advanced planning, but you may also have to install additional posts and footings if the footings are spread too far apart to fully support the railing.

HANDRAIL OPTIONS

There are about as many ways to attach handrail systems to posts as there are handrail systems. Regardless of how it attaches, a handrail system typically consists of four to six parts: the balusters, optional cap rails, the top and bottom railing, the posts, and post caps. Balusters are the vertical members of deck railing that divide up the spaces between the posts. A cap rail is an optional railing that is laid flat horizontally across the tops of posts or on top of the top rail to provide a clean appearance. The railing is the horizontal members that span the railing posts and support the balusters. The posts are structural members that attach to the rim joists and support the railing, balusters, and caps. A post cap is an accessory that fits on top of a post to give it a finished look.

How the railing system attaches to the posts depends on the system. With premade railing, the top and bottom rails typically attach to the post via short lengths of angle iron. One side attaches to the post, and the adjacent side attaches to the rail. The balusters are either screwed to the rails or fit in recesses cut in the rails. One of the advantages of this type of system is that the handrail is centered on the posts.

If your posts are mounted on the inside of the rim joists, you can install the railing centered on the post as shown in the right drawing, or slightly closer to the inside edge. The simple wood balusters can be attached directly to the rail as shown. Alternatively, you can install turned balusters between the rails. By mounting the rails slightly closer to the inside edge, you'll center the balusters better on the width of the posts.

You might want a handrail system that does not leave a gap at the bottom (as the two previous systems do). If so, and your posts are mounted to the outside of your rim joists, you can simply add a top rail and then the balusters between the top rail and the rim joist, as shown in the drawing at right.

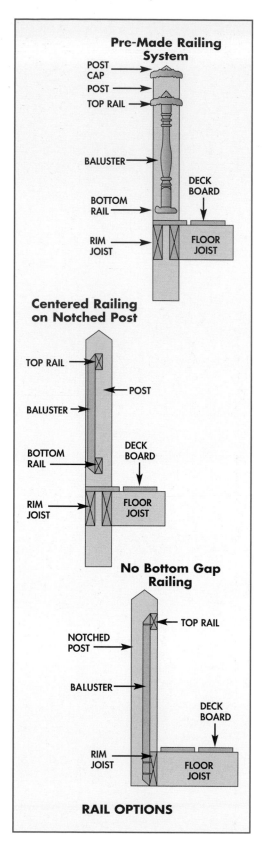

STAIR ANATOMY

■ Any deck or porch that isn't at ground level will need steps. Although you can purchase pre-made steps, odds are they weren't designed for your deck or porch. Installing stairs requires a bit of number crunching. Note that the design of the stairs will also be influenced by the materials used to construct it and by your local building codes. If your deck boards are made from composites, you should also be able to use them as treads. Note: Composites are not intended for structural use and therefore should not be used to make the stringers that support the treads.

A typical set of deck or porch stairs is shown in the drawing below. It consists of two or three stringers (the foundation of the stairs), stair treads, and optional vertical risers that close off the spaces between the treads. The stringer attaches to the deck or porch via metal joist hangers or directly to the floor or rim joists, and is fastened at the bottom to a concrete pad.

Posts usually run vertically up next to the stringers at various locations to support a handrail—something that's mandatory in many locales. The handrail consists of two or more rails spanned by balusters. The posts need to terminate in concrete footings—the size, shape, and location of which will be specified by local code. Additionally, most towns also require a concrete pad at the base of the stairs to support the stringers to prevent them from being driven into the soil with use.

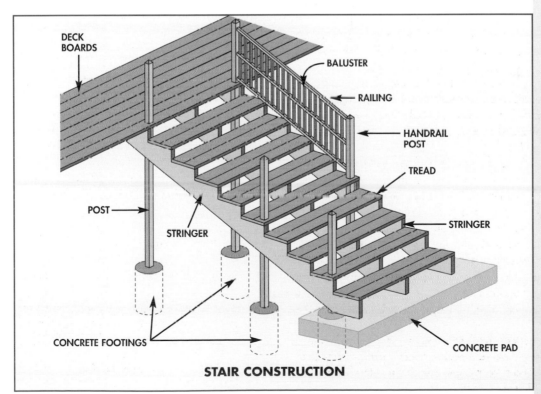

DECK BOARDS

BALUSTER

RAILING

HANDRAIL POST

TREAD

POST

STRINGER

STRINGER

CONCRETE FOOTINGS

CONCRETE PAD

STAIR CONSTRUCTION

STAIR DESIGN

■ Although somewhat complicated, stair design can be broken down into a series of simple steps (pardon the pun). In order to design your own stairs, you'll need to be familiar with stair terminology, as shown in the drawing at right.

All of the math involved in building stairs has to do with making the stringers. The first step is to establish the rise and run of the steps. The total rise is determined by measuring from the ground to the top of the deck boards or porch floor at the lowest spot. The easiest way to do this is extend a level out past the deck or porch and measure down from there.

The next step is to divide this measurement by 7" (the recommended unit rise) to determine the number of steps (round off to the nearest whole number). Now divide your measured total rise by the number of steps to determine your actual unit rise. The step run is easy to determine: If you're planning on using two 2×6's, your unit run is 10"—this allows for a gap between them and a slight overhang. Finally, you can calculate the total span (how far out the stairs will go) by multiplying the unit run by the number of treads (always one less than the number of steps).

With unit rise and unit run calculated, you can lay out the stringers. Mark the unit rise on the short leg of a framing square with tape, and the unit rise on the other leg. Start at the top of the stringer and place the framing square so tape marks align with the edge of the stringer. Trace the outline of the square on the stringer with a pencil. When you get to the bottom step, shorten the rise by the thickness of the tread material. Then go back and lay out a line 1½" below each tread. Now you can cut the notches and attach brackets if desired. After you attach the stringers, you can add the stair treads.

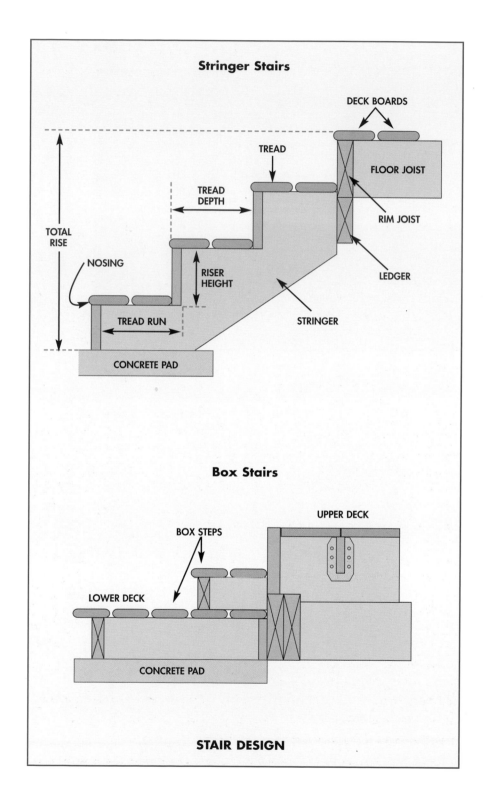

Stringer Stairs

DECK BOARDS

TREAD

FLOOR JOIST

TREAD
DEPTH

RIM JOIST

TOTAL
RISE

NOSING

RISER
HEIGHT

LEDGER

STRINGER

TREAD RUN

CONCRETE PAD

Box Stairs

UPPER DECK

BOX STEPS

LOWER DECK

CONCRETE PAD

STAIR DESIGN

PORCH ANATOMY

COMMON PORCH TERMS

Balusters – the vertical members of porch railing that divide up the space between the posts

Beam – a structural member that transfers joist loads to the posts

Columns – structural members designed to transfer the roof load to the porch foundation

Fascia – nonstructural decorative trim installed around the perimeter of a porch to cover the joists.

Flooring – typically 1×4 tongue-and-groove boards installed across the joists, perpendicular to the house

Footing – a unit (usually concrete) used to support a post to transfer the porch load to the ground

Handrail – members installed between columns or newel posts

Joist – a structural wood member that supports flooring boards and spans the joists

Knee rails – rails installed 3' above the perimeter of the porch; often used to support screening

Knee wall – a short wall around the perimeter of a porch for better appearance and added privacy

Lattice – wood strips formed into a grid that's used as screening, skirting, and overheads

Ledger – a structural member that attaches to the house and supports one end of the joists

Newel post – a member that supports a handrail where there is no column

Pier – a brick or concrete unit that supports a column, header, or beam

Post – a structural member that supports a beam and transfers the porch load to the footing

Railing – a portion of a porch designed to enclose it; typically consists of a rail post, cap rail, and balusters

Riser – the vertical portion of a step or stairway designed to support the treads

Screening – metal or fiberglass mesh installed around the perimeter of a porch to keep out insects

Skirting – a screen installed below the porch to hide the foundation and limit access

Stringer – the diagonal section of a stairway that supports the risers and treads

Tread – the horizontal portion of stairway – the step

Porches are most often built as an entrance to a house and are usually roofed. With the exception of the roof, many of the construction details of a porch are similar to that of a deck. The major differences are joist orientation and how the footings are treated. All porches have five main parts: a support system, a foundation, flooring, accessories, and usually a roof; see the drawing below and the chart at left.

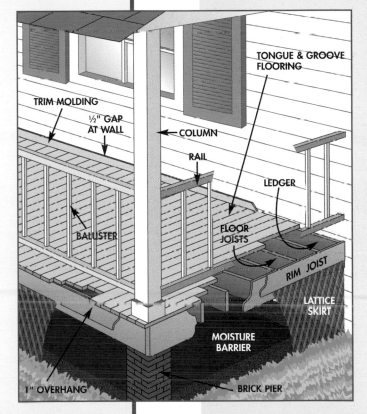

TRIM MOLDING
½" GAP AT WALL
TONGUE & GROOVE FLOORING
COLUMN
RAIL
LEDGER
BALUSTER
FLOOR JOISTS
RIM JOIST
LATTICE SKIRT
MOISTURE BARRIER
1" OVERHANG
BRICK PIER

PORCH ANATOMY,
continued

The support system. Just like a deck, the support system of a porch starts with concrete footings set into the ground. The difference here is that instead of wood posts running vertically to support the foundation, many porches utilize a brick pier or stem wall for a better appearance (see the drawing on the opposite page). The brick piers are built directly on top of the concrete footings and often have lattice or skirting that spans between the piers to hide the foundation and limit access. The opposite end of the foundation attaches to the house via a ledger board to support the flooring. Since most porches are roofed, the footings must bear the weight of the roof as well and should be designed accordingly (seek professional help for this). Stem walls are another project best left for the pros, since they require forms to define the walls and a lot of concrete. As with the piers, stem walls are often veneered with brick for a better appearance (see page 57 for more on stem walls).

The foundation. The foundation of a porch is similar to that of a deck, with one big difference—the orientation of the field joists. Unlike the field joists for a deck, which are perpendicular to the house, the field joists of a porch run parallel to the house. This is because the flooring typically runs perpendicular to the house for better drainage. The joists connect to a double 2-by beam that rests on the piers. The foundation typically slopes ¼" per foot away from the house for optimum drainage. The ground under the porch is best covered with 4-mil plastic to prevent upward migration of moisture.

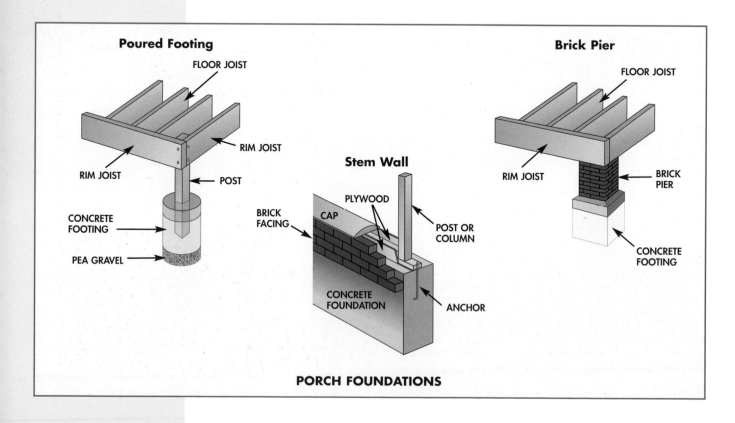

PORCH FOUNDATIONS

The flooring. The standard in porch flooring is 1×4 pressure-treated tongue-and-groove flooring. It is installed perpendicular to the house to help the porch shed water. In most cases, the flooring is painted with a high-quality porch enamel. Note that with even the best materials and optimum installation, you can expect to refinish the porch floor every 3 to 5 years, depending on local weather conditions.

Accessories. Common porch accessories include steps and a railing system that may or may not use the columns that support the roof. Since porches are such a highly visible part of a home, great care is usually taken in choosing and installing the railing system. Balusters are often turned or shaped into interesting profiles. The porch may or may not be screened.

The roof. In most cases, the porch roof is an extension of the house roof. It is supported with large columns of varying size and shape and may or may not be solid. Common shapes include box and round. For best support, the columns should rest directly over the brick piers and footings. The interior ceiling of the porch is most often covered with tongue-and-groove boards or wainscoting, and the decorative trim and molding is applied to cover gaps and serve as transitions between the roof, ceiling, and walls.

STEM WALLS AND KNEE WALLS

■ A stem wall is a poured perimeter foundation. It does a couple of things. First, it raises the structure above ground, where it will be protected from weather, insects, etc. Second, it creates a solid foundation to support porch walls and the roof. And finally, it creates a crawlspace underneath the floor for easy access to plumbing and electrical (if applicable).

The stem wall is formed by first digging a trench sufficiently wide and deep. Then forms are constructed out of lumber and plywood. Reinforcing bar is added; concrete is poured into the forms and allowed to cure before removing the forms, backfilling, and building on to the wall. Typically a length of pressure-treated pine called the mudsill is attached to the wall via a set of J-bolts that were inserted into the still-wet concrete.

A knee wall is a partial wall built on top of the stem wall. These are designed to provide privacy, but still allow plenty of fresh air. Knee walls are usually constructed out of 2-by materials and sheathed with siding to match the home. A sill on top of the knee wall slants away from the home to assist with water runoff. The knee wall may or may not be insulated.

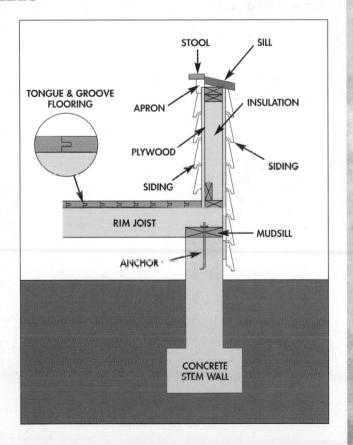

PATIO ANATOMY

■ Patios have become increasingly popular in homes across the country for two main reasons. First, many homeowners prefer the privacy of a back yard to the more public front-yard porch. Second, patios are an inexpensive add-on that home-builders can provide to enhance the value of a home.

Simple anatomy. Simplicity is the reason it's inexpensive to add on a patio. In many cases, the back patio is just a concrete slab adjacent to the home. Access is typically provided by a sliding or swinging patio door, as shown in the drawing below. And, a concrete slab is the perfect blank slate for a makeover. See pages 76–78 for examples of real patio makeovers.

Concrete slab. If the patio is a concrete slab, it will have some type of perimeter footing to anchor the slab in place. The size and depth of this footing will depend on the climate where you live. In colder areas of the country, the footing may extend below the frost line to lock the slab in place. Alternatively, some colder-climate builders use a shallow footing and allow the slab to "float." You can usually spot a shallow footing slab by its cracks.

Brick or pavers. An alternative to concrete is a brick-and-sand or paver patio. With a brick-and-sand patio, brick is either laid in a base of sand over pea gravel or laid directly on the pea gravel. When the brick is in place, sand is dumped onto the bricks and swept to fill in the cracks. With pavers, the concrete pavers are usually laid directly on a tamped bed of pea gravel. Since these pavers usually interlock, no sand or other filler is required to hold them in place.

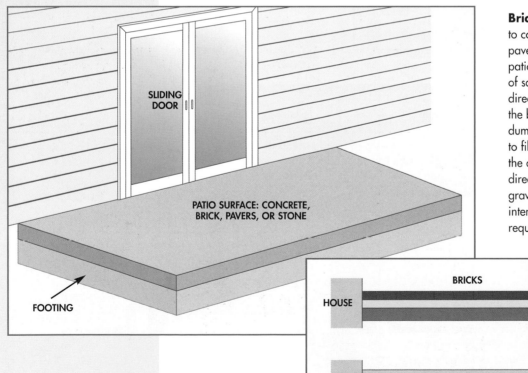

SLIDING DOOR

PATIO SURFACE: CONCRETE, BRICK, PAVERS, OR STONE

FOOTING

BRICK EDGING
BRICKS
HOUSE
Brick and Sand
PEA GRAVEL

HOUSE
SLAB
Concrete Slab
FOOTING

PATIO EDGING OPTIONS

If you decide to install brick or pavers over an existing slab or you just want to spruce up an existing patio, consider a new edging. The edging on a patio is like the frame on a picture: It can blend in or serve as an accent. The simplest edging for a concrete slab is natural landscaping, like the grass edging shown in the photo at left. If you're looking for something more decorative, there are four common ways to edge a slab or a brick or paver patio; see the drawing below. Additionally, you can use premade edging to surround a patio; see page 43 for more on this.

Edging using wood. There are two simple ways to use wood to edge a patio. The first is to attach a pressure-treated 2×4 to a pressure-treated 1×10 and bury the 1×10 partially in the ground so the 2×4 ends up flush with the patio surface. Make sure to use ground-contact-rated lumber for this. Also, to prevent frost heave, install long galvanized bolts or railroad spikes near the bottom of the 1×10 before you backfill. If you're looking for something more substantial, try edging with railroad ties. You can set them flush with the patio or let them stand proud to create a lip. Railroad spikes driven through the ties helps secure the ties. Be sure to drill holes for spikes—it's difficult to drive them through a tie without drilling first.

Edging using concrete. For a more permanent edging, use concrete. Basically you'll create a footing for the patio and set bricks in the footing to create an edging, or simply use the concrete as the edging. Different looks can be achieved by orienting the bricks flat, on their side, or on edge.

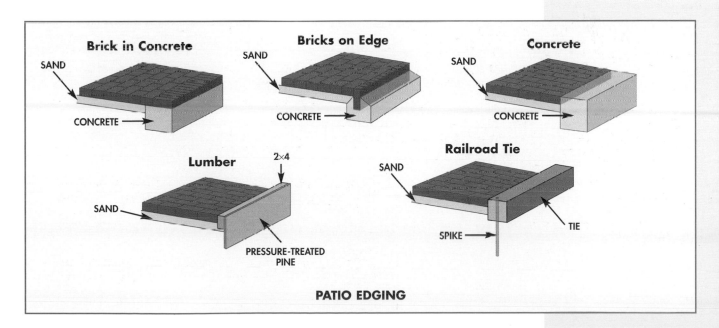

PATIO EDGING

PATIO OVERHEADS

There are two basic structural choices when adding an overhead to a deck or porch. The unit can be freestanding or attach to the house, as shown in the drawing below. Since a freestanding structure must support all of the weight of the unit, it usually consists of large beams, often with cross braces to prevent racking. A unit that attaches to the house requires only one-half the support structure, since one-half of the weight is borne by the house.

Freestanding overheads are most often pergolas or arbors and, although they do offer some shade, are mainly decorative. Depending on the region, attached overheads may be covered with shingles or corrugated roofing and angled to shed water. In areas that receive a lot of snow, any overhead needs to be designed by a professional.

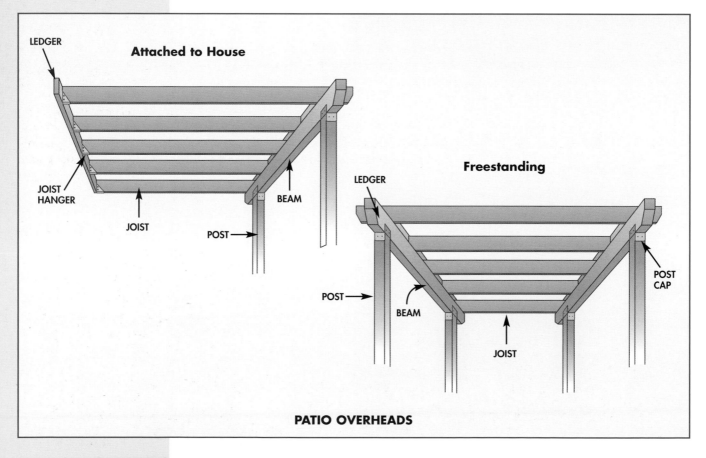

Attached to House

LEDGER

JOIST HANGER

JOIST

POST

BEAM

Freestanding

LEDGER

POST

BEAM

JOIST

POST CAP

PATIO OVERHEADS

LANDSCAPING ANATOMY

Shrub

WATERING RING CREATES MOAT FOR WATER

2"–3" MULCH

ROOT-BALL

BACKFILL:
1/2 SOIL
1/2 SOIL AMENDMENTS

HOLE = 2× WIDTH OF ROOT-BALL

SLIGHT MOUND IN CENTER PREVENTS SETTLING.

Tree

BACKFILL:
1/2 SOIL
1/2 SOIL AMENDMENTS

2"–3" MULCH

ROOT-BALL

HOLE = 2× WIDTH OF ROOT-BALL

MOUND SUPPORTS ROOT-BALL AND PREVENTS SETTLING.

LANDSCAPING CROSS-SECTION

■ Easy to overlook, but hard to overestimate when it comes to impact on your makeover: that's landscaping. It's unfortunate, because well-designed landscaping can add the distinctive details to your project that make the difference between "That's nice" and "That's gorgeous!" Although landscape design is beyond our scope here (we'll save that for another makeover book), you can get excellent advice at most home and garden centers. Bring in a rough sketch of your front, back, or side yard, and ask for suggestions (some garden centers will consult for a modest fee; others won't charge).

You can save a lot of money by doing the actual work yourself—and with help. Keep in mind that most landscaping is hard work; unless you're very fit, it's best to do the job over a couple of weekends and enlist the aid of a strong back or two.

Planting shrubs. If your landscaping plans call for new shrubs, check with your home or garden center for recommended spacing. Resist the urge to plant shrubs close together to produce an "instant" hedge or screen. This kind of crowding will hurt the plants, and your investment in them. Each shrub needs sufficient soil around it to gather nutrients. Placing them close together will cause one or more of the shrubs to starve and eventually die. For more on planting a shrub, see pages 170–171.

Planting trees. Planting a tree is a major excavation project. Keep in mind that you'll need to dig a hole that's roughly twice the width of the root-ball and as deep as it is high. After you've positioned the tree, use stakes and twine to support the tree so that it's plumb. Then backfill. Make sure to create an earthen mound around the trunk to create a watering ring; this ring helps hold in water.

U.S. HARDINESS MAP

■ For help in deciding on your new plants, trees, and shrubs, one of the best sources of information is the USDA Hardiness Zone Map, shown below. The latest version of this map, updated in 1990, shows the lowest expected temperatures in North America. On the map these temperatures are referred to as "average annual minimum temperatures" and are based on the lowest temperatures recorded for each of the years 1974 to 1986 in the United States and Canada and 1971 to 1984 in Mexico.

The map defines 10 different zones, each of which represents an area of winter hardiness for the plants of agriculture and our natural landscape. It also introduces zone 11 to represent areas that have average annual minimum temperatures above 40°F (4.4°C) and that are therefore essentially frost-free. An interactive version of this map can be found at the United States National Arboretum's website at www.usna.usda.gov/Hardzone/ushzmap.html.

How to use the map. Zones 2–10 in the map have been subdivided into light- and dark-colored sections that represent 5°F (2.8°C) differences within the 10°F (5.6°C) zone. The light color of each zone represents the colder section; the dark color, the warmer section. Zone 11 represents any area where the average annual minimum temperature is above 40°F (4.4°C).

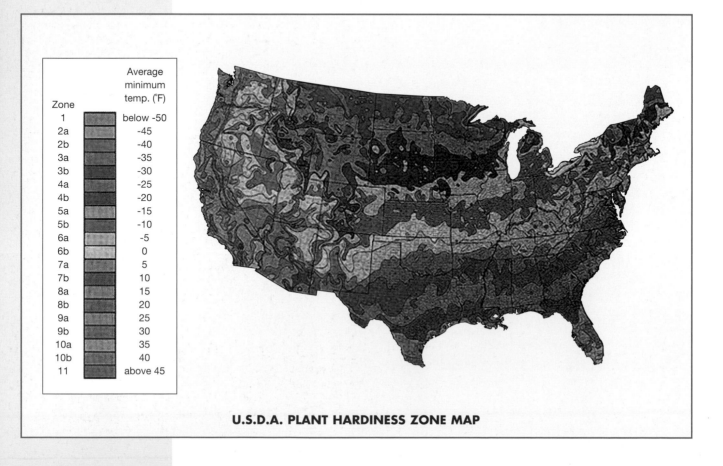

Zone	Average minimum temp. (°F)
1	below -50
2a	-45
2b	-40
3a	-35
3b	-30
4a	-25
4b	-20
5a	-15
5b	-10
6a	-5
6b	0
7a	5
7b	10
8a	15
8b	20
9a	25
9b	30
10a	35
10b	40
11	above 45

U.S.D.A. PLANT HARDINESS ZONE MAP

Real Makeover Examples

ORIGINAL DECK

HIGH-END MAKEOVER

On some TV shows, the Makeover Fairy magically transforms a space into a dream place. With a wave of the wand, poof! There's your fabulous, money-is-no-object makeover, all in the space of 30 minutes. For those of us who don't have such magical helpers, improving a deck, porch, or patio requires a true reality check: How much do we have to spend—and what can we get for those dollars?

That's exactly what you'll see in these pages: a deck, porch, and patio owned by real people with actual budget limits, and the changes that can be made. We gave each outdoor space a triple makeover to show what you can achieve at three spending levels: economy, mid-range, and high-end.

For all three outdoor areas, you'll find a photo of the space before and after, a list of the improvements made, and approximate costs. Since the deck, porch, and patio received three makeovers apiece, all distinctive, you'll browse through nine makeovers in all: different looks, different projects, and different budgets.

Maybe you'll love one look, or choose elements from a few different ones for your own deck, porch, or patio. Without any magic wand, you'll stamp your personal style on your own MoneySmart Makeover.

ORIGINAL DECK

This original, 25-year-old structure was a case study in what happens to a wooden deck when maintenance is ignored. Years of unprotected exposure to the elements left it looking raw, discolored, and just plain shabby. At first glance, you might think the only option is to rip it down and start all over—a costly venture, and a full-scale remodeling job.

There was even more than an eyesore here, though: This deck of pressure-treated pine was a hazard, too. Warped boards, nail pops, and rickety balusters made it a risky place for children, pets, and bare feet (or paws) of any age.

On the plus side, the footings and pressure-treated foundation were still in solid shape, so a complete teardown wasn't necessary. Another plus: The owners liked the tiered design. So, we were able to retain the underlying structure, and concentrate our makeover efforts on the elements that show: flooring, railings, posts, and steps.

ECONOMY DECK

What a difference a stain makes: The transformation from worn-and-weathered to rich-and-warm took just a few cans of Thompson's Water Seal products, plus ready-made posts, balusters, and railings from a local home center.

For our economy makeover, we first removed the rickety old railing system entirely. This was also a good time to repair and replace damaged deck boards.

The next step was to erase decades of grime with Thompson's deck cleaner, a pre-mixed, brush-on cleaner that rinses off. A coating of Thompson's stain quickly imbued the old boards with a handsome new tone (the newer line of tinted waterproofers can be applied just 2 hours after cleaning). It all took just a few hours and just a bit over $100. Finally, the pre-made railing system of natural cedar completed the low-cost makeover. Instead of trying to match the color of the deck surface, we opted to tint and seal the new railing system a lighter, accent shade. We could have spent thousands, but didn't—and we still achieved a fresh, attractive look.

WHAT WE DID

Cleaned deck ($50)

Repaired/replaced deck boards ($75)

Installed new rail system ($400)

Stained deck and rail system ($75)

Total cost: $350 – $500, depending on materials selected and size of deck

MID-RANGE DECK

Because its foundation was still sturdy, our once-ugly "deck"-ling was a prime candidate for the next, mid-range makeover step: a vinyl deck covering. This retrofit system from Durable Deck installs right over existing wood (or concrete) to give a slip-resistant, no-maintenance deck. Because it fits over existing surfaces, no teardowns, disposal costs, or permits are necessary.

Installation is fairly easy (the system was designed to be homeowner-friendly): You cut the planks to length and literally screw them to your existing deck. (A clever snap-in strip even conceals the screws.) This system has air channels for circulation and evaporation; we liked the textured surface for added safety underfoot. Trim that's color-matched to any of the several shades available lets you conceal deck and stair edges. We chose a neutral flooring color, sparked by the crisp white railing system.

With the addition of some minor landscaping (blue holly shrubs and ornamental grass), this deck looks brand new and ready for leisure time.

WHAT WE DID

Installed deck cover ($800)

Covered stair and fascia ($300)

Installed new rail system ($600)

Simple landscaping ($100)

Total cost: $1,500 – $2,000, depending on materials selected and size of deck

HIGH-END DECK

The adage "you get what you pay for" certainly holds true for our high-end, pull-out-the-stops deck. Yes, the quality wood composite decking from TimberTech costs more than some alternatives, but it's tough to beat for durability and maintenance-free good looks.

The material itself (a blend of wood and cellulose materials with virgin plastic) looks like natural wood, but is non-skid and splinter-free. It comes in three colors (ditto the matching rail system, plus white), and you can stain or paint it if you like. Since this is replacement material, we first removed the old decking, and installed the TimberTech planks, cutting them to fit and securing them to the joists. After covering the stairs and trim pieces, we installed the railing system—same material, different color for contrast. Note: You need at least 12" clearance from the bottom of the joist to the ground to use most composites successfully.

For a more finished look and extra safety, we added a stair railing. Gleaming copper post caps give a suitably "dressed-up" look to this grand finale. Anyone for cocktails on the deck?

WHAT WE DID

Removed old decking ($0)

Installed composite decking ($3,000)

Covered stair and trim ($400)

Installed composite railing ($2,500)

Total cost: $6,000 – $8,000, depending on materials selected and size of deck

MAKEOVER DETAILS

The success of a makeover often depends on attention to details. In the high-end deck shown here, these details are matching accessories (composite railing and matching trim), deck boards with hidden fasteners, and highly polished copper caps.

Accessories. In years past, the only composite deck parts available were deck boards. Now savvy manufacturers have created matching or complementary accessories to blend well with their deck boards, like the TimberTech railing system in the top photo.

Worry-free decking. Imagine walking barefoot across the long deck shown below without ever having to worry about catching on splinters, or protruding fasteners. That's just one of the advantages of TimberTech deck planks.

Copper caps. One of the true distinctive touches of the high-end deck makeover are the copper post caps shown above. Not only do these look good, but they also protect the posts from the elements.

ORIGINAL PORCH

■ Some porches say "Welcome"; this one barely mutters "This way in." It's functional, sure, but no more than that: There's a roof overhang for shelter, an old screen/storm door, a plain window, and a stained, cracked concrete floor. Bare and spartan, this "before" offered lots of "after" potential. Its good-sized floor space was unused, and just begged for some seating and plants. Here, the overhang was key: deep enough not just to hold some furniture, but also to let people sit a spell and enjoy being outdoors, rain or shine.

With this ideal blank slate, almost any design motif could be called on to add grace, warmth, and style. In fact, that was the owners' dilemma: What should they do, what could they do, to spruce up this space? First, we identified the three spending brackets that were feasible. Then, we homed in on three broad "looks"—country, casual, and the all-purpose eclectic, and the projects that would achieve the varied effects.

ECONOMY PORCH

■ With little more than paint, pre-made scrollwork and plants, the once stark space becomes an inviting place to linger, and a charming introduction to the home. Happily, this big change was possible with improvements that were almost totally cosmetic, and fairly inexpensive.

The lone pillar becomes a focal point of our economy makeover with the lightweight gingerbread trim that takes paint easily to match the newly painted walls. Suggesting Victorian wood elegance, this ornamentation is actually a urethane foam product from the folks at Fypon. New, burgundy-toned shutters help the window stand out, instead of disappear, and lead the eye to the wrought-iron bistro set waiting for a party of two.

A coach lamp–style light illuminates a planter, a cheerful hanging plant, and the outdoor rug that defines the sitting space. We painted the trim a soft coral to warm up the bright, white freshness of the walls. For just a few hours' work and little money, the porch that was blah is now beautiful.

WHAT WE DID

Painted walls ($50)

Painted trim ($10)

Painted door ($10)

New porch light ($75)

Added ornamentation ($100)

Added shutters ($50)

Outdoor area rug ($125)

Total cost: $200 – $420, depending on materials selected and size of porch

MID-RANGE PORCH

■ What can you do with a little more money and time? Here's just one answer: The makeover headline here is the addition of a side railing. This wooden rail, commonly available at home centers, increases a feeling of privacy at the entryway—and, it offers a perfect perch for a planter and colorful blooms. (We built the planter on-site, but you can easily find one ready-made.)

A pale yellow paint on the walls looks cheerful and fresh, contrasting with the green of the indoor/outdoor carpeting. A wall medallion of faux stone partners with a modern-style light fixture to extend the casual theme.

We painted the shutters gray, and picked up that shade in the gray/green of the glider seat's striped fabric. In all, our mid-range makeover suggests casual, easy living—and there's still room for a small side table or umbrella stand. Change the shades of paint and carpet and select another type of seating, and you can readily customize this look to your own preferences.

WHAT WE DID

Painted walls ($50)

Painted trim ($10)

Installed shutters ($50)

New storm door ($200)

Installed wood handrail ($125)

Site-built planter ($20)

Indoor/outdoor carpeting ($200)

Total cost: $500 – $700, depending on materials selected and size of porch

HIGH-END PORCH

■ Style and substance: This high-end version is all about materials in two keys areas: the railing and the door. The porch railing is still there, but we replaced it with a TimberTech wood composite railing that needs no paint, stain, or maintenance to keep its clean good looks for a long time. Yes, it costs more, and gives splinter-free beauty in exchange. The door, such a visible part of any porch, really needed replacing to keep up with the rest of the porch. Here, we invested a bit more money to get a full-view, leaded glass door, with lustrous brass hardware to match the storm door.

Paint again shows the impact of color: We painted the walls a peachy tan, the trim, white for accent, and the shutters, Hunter green. The concrete floor, which started out stained and cracked, got some fill work and a fresh coat of pale gray paint. Style fans will note the Mission-look light, which casts a classic glow on the equally classic mahogany garden bench (the owner's personal, favorite touch), flanked by an all-season planter. Now, the home's first impression is sleek, comfortable, and very inviting.

WHAT WE DID

Painted walls ($50)

Painted trim ($10)

Painted floor ($50)

Added shutters ($50)

New exterior door ($500)

Installed composite railing ($500)

New porch light ($100)

Total cost: $1,100 – $1,500, depending on materials selected and size of porch

ORIGINAL PATIO

■ It's mostly level, in one piece, and bordered by a stately, flowering plum tree. Those are the chief assets of this concrete slab patio, a common (and commonly plain) way to enjoy the outdoors. While there's nothing horribly wrong with this space, it could be so much more, and more comfortable.

Sited on the western side of the home, this patio is completely exposed to afternoon sun—a squinty proposition much of the year, and uncomfortable in the heat of summer. Depending on the weather and the season, the owners found they couldn't really use the space for relaxing and entertaining as much as they'd like. And, they knew that it didn't offer much eye appeal.

The slab itself, while structurally sound, needed cosmetic help. Small leaves had drifted onto the concrete when it was first poured, leaving a pattern of dark, I-thought-I-swept-those-up marks everywhere. With these factors in mind, we focused on two priorities: creating more shelter from the sun, without totally blocking out the sky, and finding ways to conceal the blemishes in the concrete.

ECONOMY PATIO

To tackle the first priority—shelter from the afternoon sun—we installed a corrugated vinyl roof that lets light in but keeps glare out. Still wide open to breezes, the patio now seems more like transition space between the home and the back yard, instead of just yard. The roof and support posts were deliberately positioned to keep a margin of concrete "bare" for yard work and muddy feet.

With minor repairs to give the concrete a uniformly flat look and feel, the economy patio was ready for its instant cover-up: indoor/outdoor carpeting. Not only does the carpet define the area devoted to relaxing and dining, but it gives barefooted ease to those who gather there.

The finishing touch, courtesy of the experts at Biddle Outdoor Center, Sedona/Prescott Arizona (www.biddleoutdoorcenter.com), is a handsome suite of patio furniture and accessories. Made of powder-coated steel, with dyed-through acrylic, sun-resistant fabric, the pieces are at the affordable end of fine outdoor goods, and they'll last for years. While you can pick up bargain furniture almost anywhere, invest in quality if at all possible for patio pieces. "The good stuff" really holds up against the elements.

WHAT WE DID

Repaired concrete pad ($25)

Added indoor/outdoor carpeting ($250)

Installed corrugated roof ($400)

Total cost: $600 – $800, depending on materials selected and size of patio

MID-RANGE PATIO

■ Who couldn't picture themselves lounging on this upgraded, mid-range patio? Overhead, we replaced the corrugated roof with an elegant pergola (or arbor) of pressure-treated pine slats. This helps reduce the "squint factor" in the afternoons, while still letting light and air flow freely. And, it differentiates this almost-outdoor space from the surrounding yard.

Underfoot, an all-weather area rug complements the terra cotta tones of the painted pergola, and picks up the spice tones of the pillows. Again, floor textiles define the space, add color, and are barefoot-friendly. Change the colors of the textiles, and you can dramatically change the look of this patio.

Another way to add visual drama: the furnishings. These chairs, settee, and tables are crafted of jarrah wood, a teak-like lumber from Australia. Unavailable in the United States until about 10 years ago, this line, provided by Biddle Outdoor Center, will age as you prefer. An oil coating will keep the deep cocoa brown tone, or you can skip the oil and let it gradually weather to a rustic, grayish shade. Where winters are harsh, covers are recommended for fine outdoor pieces.

WHAT WE DID

Added area rug ($300)
Installed attached pergola ($800)
Painted pergola ($75)

Total cost: $1,100 – $1,400, depending on materials selected and size of patio

HIGH-END PATIO

■ Forget the patio—how about a whole new sunroom? This seriously high-end makeover is possible with a do-it-yourself, enclosed sunroom kit from SunPorch Structures, Inc. (www.sunporch.com). In colder months, the removable windows provide insulation, and preserve solar warmth. When it gets hot, you pop out the windows, and let the screens (and interior pleated shades) keep you cool. With no change to the "footprint" of the patio (no permit needed, in many locales), we created a three- or four-season living space. Doors on both sides offer easy access to this comfortable retreat.

Just as high-end looking: the porcelain tile flooring we installed on top of the concrete pad. Rated for exterior use (a must), this extra touch was surprisingly affordable.

Surprisingly easy-care is the deluxe furniture from Biddle Outdoor Center: It isn't wicker, but an all-weather resin that won't splinter or crack. Topped with tropical print fabric that's made of sun-resistant synthetic, these pieces will keep their color and beauty for years. Dirty footprints or spilled drinks? Just hose them off.

This finale may be a bit too grand for some budgets, but if you've priced putting an addition on your home, you know that this option could be a smart and versatile alternative.

WHAT WE DID

Installed sunroom ($9,000)

Tiled patio floor ($300)

Total cost: $8,000 – $12,000, depending on materials selected and size of patio

Creating Your New Look

We didn't use magic wands to create the makeovers in these pages, and neither will you. That's why, in this section, you'll get down to the nuts and bolts (or screws and paintbrushes) of how to actually create your new look.

What needs upgrading around your place: the deck? Porch? Patio? Whatever your target, we'll show you step-by-step how to do the projects in this book. From staining a deck to installing outdoor tile, you'll find the techniques that work— and tips that help make the job go smoother and faster.

We've divided the projects into the major categories involved: decks, porches, patios, floors, exterior doors, and final touches. Each starts with an "after" photo showing the payoff of the tasks involved. Each project also includes in-process photos, plus a list of the tools that you'll need. This is the fun part: your own MoneySmart Makeover.

DECKS

Over the years, decks have increasingly replaced the front porch. Homeowners aren't as interested in socializing with their neighbors on the front porch as they are in capturing a few moments of quiet time alone on the back deck, or entertaining a select group privately, away from the busy street. But porches had an advantage over decks: They were usually covered. And this meant the floor and most of the porch was protected from the elements.

The typical deck, however, is totally exposed and so will degrade faster because of the constant barrage of wind, sun, rain, and snow. That's why the deck is such a popular choice for a makeover. Sprucing up your deck is a rewarding way to spend a lovely spring or summer afternoon. Makeover projects in this chapter range from simple cleaning and re-staining to removing old deck boards and replacing them with new composite decking.

Common Deck Problems

Anyone who's considering a deck makeover is already aware of the reasons behind their thinking: The deck obviously needs help. When a deck looks old and worn out, it may just be cosmetic—or there may be structural issues you need to be aware of. Here are some of the more common problems you should look for. When you find any of these, they should be taken care of before proceeding to the cosmetics.

Bad deck boards. Next to nail pop, the second most frequent problem you'll find on an older deck is bad deck boards, as shown in the photo at left. These are boards that are warped, twisted, rotted, or broken. With the exception of a warped deck board, all the other problems will require you to replace the board; see page 84 for more on this. If the board is warped but in good condition, see page 83 for a technique to straighten the board. Discolored boards often only need a cleaning; see pages 86–87.

Nail pop. Probably the most common problem with an old deck is nail "pop." The wood boards on old decks are often secured with nails, and nails are prone to popping throughout the year. What happens is this: As the seasons change, the wood expands and contracts. This constant in and out movement of the wood effectively squeezes or pushes the nail up and out of the wood, as shown in the photo above left. There are two cures for this: one temporary, the other more permanent.

Bad railings. Compared to horizontal deck boards, railings don't generally take as tough a beating from the elements, since they're vertical. Still, they're often subject to much more stress, as people lean against them or sit on them. Any one of the three main components of the railing can fail: The rails can warp or twist, the balusters can warp or break (as shown in the photo at right), and the posts can crack under use. See page 85 for how to replace rails and balusters.

Straightening Deck Boards

TOOLS

- Hammer
- Cat's paw
- Driver/drill and bits

A deck that's in reasonable condition can often get a fresh new look with a thorough cleaning and painting or staining (see pages 86–87 and 88–89, respectively). Older decks, however, will generally need some TLC before cleaning and staining. In particular, the wood deck boards will likely have warped over time. If the deck boards are in good shape, it's a relatively painless task to straighten them. (If the boards are in bad shape, they'll need to be replaced; see page 84 for how to do this.)

Remove fasteners as needed. To straighten a deck board, start by removing the nails or screws that hold down the end of the warped board. Screws are backed out using a driver/drill fitted with a screwdriver bit. Nails can be more of a challenge unless they've "popped" over time (see page 82). In most cases, the nail heads will be flush or slightly below the surface of the deck board. The best tool to remove these types of nails is a cat's paw. This special prybar has a set of claws on a curved end that can be driven into the wood so they slip under the nail's head. Then you just pry out the nail, as shown in the bottom left photo.

Straighten the board. Now you can straighten the board; all you need is a couple of scrap-wood wedges and a hammer. Just tap the wedges between the warped board and the deck board next to it to straighten out the board from which you removed the nails (top photo). The board may straighten with a single wedge, or you might need to use several. Alternatively, the folks at Cepco Tools (www.cepco-tool.com) make a nifty deck board straightener called the BoWrench. The best thing about this tool is that once you've used it to straighten a board, you can let it go, and it holds the board in place while you secure it. The leverage action is so strong with this tool that you can even straighten several boards at once.

Secure the board with screws. Once you've straightened the board, you can secure it to the joists with screws as shown in the bottom right photo. You could use nails here, but the screws will do a much better job of holding the board in place over time.

Replacing Deck Boards

A loose, twisted, or damaged deck board is one of the most common problems with a wood deck. For a loose board, try driving in a screw or two at an angle. If you drive them in at opposing angles, the screws will lock the board to the joist. Make sure to use galvanized or stainless steel screws. To minimize the visual impact of the screw, use a trim-head screw. We don't recommend using nails at all here, as they just don't have the holding power that the threads of a screw offer.

Add cleat to joist and secure. In most cases, it's a good idea to add additional support under the deck board to create a more stable foundation. Measure and cut a scrap of wood to fit under the deck board. Then attach it directly to the joist with screws, as shown in the top photo. Make sure to use pressure-treated lumber or a hardy exterior wood like the cedar shown here.

Install new boards. After you've added a cleat, next measure, mark, and cut a replacement board to length. Position the replacement deck board so there's an equal gap on each side, and then attach it to the underlying joists (and cleat) with galvanized or stainless steel screws, as shown in the bottom right photo. Drill pilot holes near the ends of the replacement board to prevent the board from splitting when the screw is driven in.

Remove old boards. If you find a board that is beyond repair, you'll need to replace it. In most cases you can pry it up with a prybar or crowbar as shown in the photo above left. If the damage is limited to one end of a long board, cut through the board directly over and centered above a joist, as near as possible to the damage. (A reciprocating saw fitted with a demolition blade is the best tool for this.) Then pry out the damaged section.

Repairing Railings and Balusters

Although railings and balusters tend to take less abuse than deck boards because they're mostly vertical instead of horizontal, they can and will require some attention over time. Part of your deck makeover may entail removing and replacing some of the railing or balusters.

Replace top railing. Because rails are horizontal, they often require more attention than the balusters. In many cases, the railings are either 1-by or 2-by material, so replacement is a simple matter of prying off the old piece and installing a new one.

If the railing is shaped, it's best to use the old part as a template to make the new one. Measure and cut a rail to size and shape and attach it to the existing posts using weather-resistant screws, as shown in the photo above left.

Remove the old baluster. How difficult or easy it is to replace a damaged baluster will depend on your railing system. On systems like the one shown here, where the baluster attaches to the railing, replacement is easy. If the baluster is screwed in place, back out the screws to remove it; otherwise

pull it off by hand or with a crowbar. For systems where the baluster attaches to top and bottom rails, you'll need to cut through the fasteners in order to pull out the baluster. A mini-hacksaw like the one shown in the photo at right works well for this, as does a reciprocating saw fitted with a demolition blade.

Install the new baluster. Measure the length of an existing baluster (or the damaged one if it's in one piece), and transfer this measurement to a replacement baluster. Cut the replacement to length and check the fit. Before you install the new baluster, it's a good idea to brush on a coat or two of preservative to the top and bottom of the baluster to help protect it from moisture damage. Next, drill pilot holes in the baluster for the fasteners you'll be using to attach it—this extra step will help prevent

splitting as the screws are driven in. Now you can position the baluster centered between its neighbors and attach it with galvanized or stainless steel screws (bottom photo).

Cleaning a Deck

Sometimes all it takes to make over a deck is to clean it thoroughly. Cleaning a deck like this is like flossing your teeth: You've got to get between deck boards, railings, and balusters to remove debris that can cause rot and decay, just as food trapped between teeth can cause tooth decay and cavities. The sequence is simple and effective.

The entire job, including optional pressure-washing (highly recommended), will take less than a few hours. It's time well spent to keep your deck looking new and structurally sound.

Prepare the area. Since most of the deck-cleaning chemicals you'll be likely to use contain some form of acid, the next step is to mask off the house to prevent the acid from discoloring the exterior of the house (photo above). You'll also want to protect nearby plants and shrubs with drop cloths or plastic to prevent damage. The same applies to your railing if you're not cleaning it. Any sprayover or droplets can discolor an existing finish.

Sweep away debris. The first step to cleaning a deck is to sweep it well to remove any loose debris. A stiff-bristle "garage"-style broom works best (above photo). Pay particular attention to deck areas where parts butt up against each other. These collect debris and are some of the areas most susceptible to rot and decay. That's because the debris traps water, which promotes the growth of mold, mildew, and fungus. This is very common on decks where the balusters run all the way to the deck boards, such as the one shown here.

PRESSURE-WASHERS

When it comes to cleaning a deck that's heavily stained or has a lot of caked-on dirt and grime, it's a good idea to pressure-wash the deck before applying a chemical cleaner. Pressure-washing helps loosen stubborn dirt and lets you blow debris out of corners and crevices. If you don't own a pressure-washer, you can pick one up for a day at most rental centers. The best method is to start in the center of the deck and work your way out toward both ends.

Spray on a cleaner. Now you're ready to apply the cleaner or brightener. Usually, the easiest way to apply it is with a pump garden sprayer, as shown in the top photo. Wear gloves, and read and follow the manufacturer's directions: Some want you to apply the chemical to a dry deck surface, while others want it wet. Also, some do not recommend using a garden sprayer and instead suggest you apply the product with a brush or roller. In any case, take care to apply it only where you want to clean and lighten wood.

Scrub the deck. Although most chemical cleaners say you don't need to scrub the deck, you're sure to find spots or stains that would benefit from a little elbow grease. Most home centers sell brooms especially intended for cleaning decks—they typically have a short head and long, stiff bristles. Note that really stubborn stains may require several applications of cleaner followed by brisk scrubbing with the broom, as shown in the middle photo.

Rinse off the deck. After you've waited the time specified by the manufacturer of the cleaner you're using, you can rinse off the deck. Apply lots of water using a hose fitted with a sprayer attachment, as shown in the bottom photo. Rinse the deck completely and then go back and rinse it again. Allow the deck to totally dry before staining or painting (if desired).

Staining or Painting a Deck

Want an instant deck makeover? Apply a fresh coat of stain or paint; just make sure the deck is clean first (pages 86–87) and in good repair (pages 82–85). A fresh finish is also the best way to increase the lifespan of your deck and keep it looking good. How often you need to reapply a finish to your deck depends on its finish and the local weather conditions. Likewise, the type of finish you use will affect the frequency of maintenance. Transparent water sealants need to be refreshed every year, while stains may need attention less frequently. Though most composite decking doesn't require a finish, many of them will accept one—just realize that once you apply one, the finish will need regular attention.

Prepare the deck area. The first thing you'll read on the directions of any can of deck finish is that the deck must be clean and free from dirt. If your deck is in fairly good shape, you may be able to get by with just a thorough sweeping. If the deck is stained and dirty, you'll need to do a more complete cleaning, which may or may not include pressure-washing and the use of a chemical cleaner; see pages 86–87 for more on this. Note that most finishes require a surface that's totally dry. Depending on how you'll be applying the deck finish, you may want to mask off sensitive areas of the deck (like the exterior walls). It is also wise to protect nearby plants and shrubs with drop cloths or plastic (middle photo). This is particularly important when spraying on a finish with a garden sprayer or an air-powered paint sprayer. It's also important to check the deck to make sure it will absorb the finish. Most finish directions will instruct you to apply water first to see how well it absorbs into the deck (inset photo).

Spray on the finish.

Now you're ready to apply the finish. Follow the manufacturer's directions for number of coats and application. Some finishes are best applied with a garden sprayer, as shown in the top left photo. Some manufacturers recommended applying the stain with a short nap roller to get an even coat. This way, when the inevitable puddling occurs, you can spread the finish out to prevent darker staining in these areas. Although it's easy to concentrate on the flat horizontal surfaces of a deck, don't forget to protect the ends of deck boards by brushing on a couple of coats of finish. Sealing the ends of the boards is one of the best ways to prevent the board from soaking up moisture that can cause it to split, cup, and twist. Wipe on several coats, allowing the finish to soak up into the ends between applications.

Brush finish on the railings.

Although you can spray a finish onto the railings, you'll find that you'll end up spraying a lot of excess finish onto either your deck or your lawn. That's why we recommend applying finish to the railing with a brush, as shown in the photo above. This method ensures an even coat (which is hard to do when spraying), and it eliminates any overspray issues.

Use a paint pad for the fascia.

The fascia (the trim that runs around the perimeter of the deck and is attached to the rim joists) can also be finished with a brush, but you'll find that a paint pad fitted with a short nap will make quick work of the job, as shown in the top right photo. When you purchase one of these for the fascia, stay away from the foam varieties: These tend to tear easily when they encounter a stray splinter or lifted edge, which is very common in wood exposed to the outdoors.

Wipe off the excess finish.

As you complete each section of the deck—the deck boards, the railing, and the fascia and trim—take the time to wipe off any excess stain. This not only will remove any drips, but it also prevent some areas from darkening more than others, as shown in the bottom right photo. Also, whether or not you'll need to apply a second coat of finish will really depend on the type of finish and the level of protection you're after. Follow the manufacturer's directions to the letter here because the old adage "more is better" does not always apply. Many deck finishes are formulated for one-coat coverage, and laying down another coat may actually harm your deck. This is especially true with finishes designed to let your deck boards "breathe" as they react to changes in humidity.

Deck Demolition

There will be occasions when a deck makeover simply calls for new decking. The old boards may be in such bad shape that it would make more sense to replace them all instead of trying to patch the deck. In most cases, this means removing the old deck boards. The exception to this is if you're planning on installing a deck cover as shown on pages 92–95.

Remove the railings. Since most decks have a railing system, the first step in removing a deck is to remove the existing railing. Splinters are highly likely here, so make sure to protect your hands with leather gloves. Begin by pulling out any popped nails (see page 82), as shown in the bottom left photo. Then remove other nails as needed with a cat's paw. Now you should be able to lift off the top railing (inset).

Remove the balusters and posts. Removing the top rail will expose the balusters in most cases. Just grip these with both hands and pry them off the bottom rail. Then remove the bottom rail. All that's left of the railing should be the posts. To remove these, start by loosening and removing all mounting hardware. Then grab the post and pull it away from the rim joist as shown in the top right photo. Repeat for all the posts.

Remove the deck boards. The deck boards usually come up fairly easily if persuaded with a crowbar or prybar, as shown in the bottom right photo. Take care here, as you'll encounter plenty of exposed nails. Set the planks aside in a roped-off area to keep kids and pets away from the exposed nails. Continue until all the deck boards have been removed. Then carefully inspect each of the joists for stray fasteners; remove any that you find.

Installing Wood Decking

Even though there are a number of materials options available for deck boards, many homeowners still prefer the look of wood. Besides, wood deck boards are still the least expensive covering you can put on your deck. If you do install new deck boards, take the time to protect your investment by staining or painting the wood to help it hold up better against the elements.

Install the first plank. To install wood deck boards, start at the rim joist and work back toward the house. Measure, mark, and cut the first deck board to length. Don't worry about aligning the end of the board: Allow it to "run wild"—you'll trim it later. We recommend screws when it's time to attach deck boards, as shown in the bottom left photo. Sure, nails are faster, but they just don't have the holding power that screws offer. Depending on the material, you may need to drill pilot holes. Regardless of the material, it's always a good idea to drill pilot holes near the end of the board to prevent splitting.

Stagger the planks. How big the gap should be between the deck boards will depend on the material you use. The standard for years was to insert 16d nails between boards, as shown in the bottom right photo. This might look nice when the deck is laid, but if you're using pressure-treated wood, the deck boards will likely shrink considerably over time. You best bet here is to butt the boards up against each other and fasten them to the joists. As you lay the second course of planks, make sure to stagger the ends of the boards so they don't all line up over the same joist (inset). Finally, when all the deck boards are in place, you can tidy up any overhanging or "wild" ends by trimming them all at once. Snap a chalk line indicating the desired overhang (if any), and use a circular saw to carefully remove the wild ends. Make sure to cut on the waste side of the line. Finish off the cuts near the ledger with a handsaw or reciprocating saw.

Installing a Deck Cover

So your deck's in good shape but looks terrible. What do you do? Sure, you could pressure-wash it and stain or paint it, but then you'd have to do the same thing next year...and the year after...and so on. Why not give your old deck a fresh new look by installing a deck cover (like the one shown in the top photo)? The vinyl deck cover consists of a set of thin extruded planks (see below) that are screwed directly to your existing deck. Vinyl trim wraps around the deck, and when fascia trim is added, you'll never know the old deck is there. Adding a vinyl handrail (see pages 176–178) creates a pristine deck with no exposed fasteners, plus the added advantage of no maintenance. You'll need to do no more painting or staining; just hose the deck cover off periodically to keep it clean.

Simply wrap this around the corner, using screws to secure it as you go.

Deck cap. The deck cover we used here, by Durable Deck (www.durabledeck.com), comes in 12', 16', and 20' lengths of extruded vinyl. The underlying fins of the extrusion fully support foot traffic. And the two slotted grooves in each plank accept stainless steel or galvanized screws to secure the plank to the deck, as shown in the drawing. Thin snap-in cover strips or caps fit into the grooves to conceal the screws, providing a surface free from fasteners.

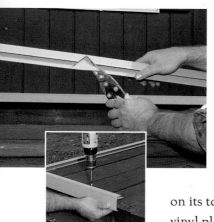

Install the edging. The first step to installing a vinyl deck cover is to attach the perimeter trim as shown in the inset photo. This trim has a C-shaped channel on its top edge to accept the vinyl planks. Attach the trim to the deck edge with stainless steel or galvanized screws. When it comes time to go around a corner, cut a 90-degree notch in the top edge of the trim as shown in the photo above.

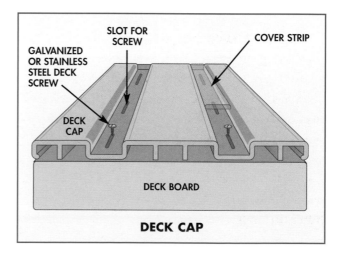

GALVANIZED OR STAINLESS STEEL DECK SCREW

SLOT FOR SCREW

COVER STRIP

DECK CAP

DECK BOARD

DECK CAP

Prepare the deck boards. With all the trim in place, the next step is to carefully inspect the entire surface of the deck for old fasteners that have "popped" or risen above the surface. With a hammer, pound down any that you find, as shown in the top photo. Better yet, remove the nail and replace it with a screw. The last thing you want is an old deck fastener rising and causing a lump in the deck cover, which could eventually lead to damage to the plank.

Install the planks. How you install the planking will depend on the pattern you're after. Durable Deck recommends running the planks perpendicular to or (as shown here) diagonal to the existing wood deck boards. Carefully measure the length of the first plank and cut it to length, mitering the ends if desired. (A power miter saw fitted with a 40- to 60-tooth carbide-tipped blade is the best tool for cutting the vinyl—make sure to wear protective eyewear, as the brittle vinyl can shatter occasionally when cut.) Slip the first plank into the channels in the perimeter trim. Secure the plank to the deck with stainless steel or galvanized screws every 9" along the length of the plank, as shown in the middle photo. Continue measuring, cutting, and screwing successive planks in place until the deck is covered (inset photo).

Add the cover strip. With all the planks in place, you can install the cover strips or trim caps to conceal the screws holding down the planks. Use a rubber mallet to snap the cover strips into the grooves in the planks, as shown in the bottom photo. Don't be tempted to use a hammer here—these strips are easily damaged if struck by a metal hammer. Cut the cover strips to length and miter the ends if needed.

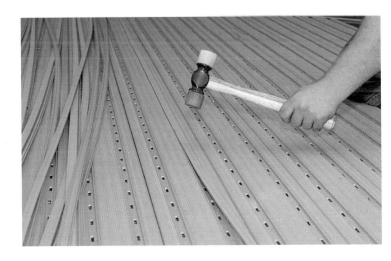

Fascia: Install the trimmed piece. After the deck is covered, you can go around the perimeter and cover the rim joists with the same planking materials used to cover the deck. To do this, first temporarily hold a plank so it's flush with the bottom edge of the rim joists. Then measure the section that's not covered. In most cases, you'll need to rip a plank to width to fit in the space. For best appearance, consider mitering the ends of the fascia pieces where they come together at the corners. Once you've cut the piece to width and length, install it first, as shown in the top photo.

Fascia: Install the planks. With the trimmed piece in place, go ahead and measure and cut a plank to fit underneath the trimmed piece, as shown in the middle photo. Repeat this process, first cutting a trimmed piece and installing it before attaching a full-width plank for the uncovered sides of the deck.

Fascia: Cover the corner. If you don't want to miter the ends of the fascia piece, an alternative method is to install them by simply butting the ends together. Then you can cover the exposed extrusion with a piece of 90-degree corner trim, as shown in the bottom photo. You can either screw this piece to the rim joists or secure it with silicone caulk. In either case, finish off the fascia by measuring and trimming cover strips to length and snapping them in the plank grooves with a rubber mallet.

Wood steps can also be covered with vinyl deck planks. The idea here is to basically treat each step as if it were a tiny, three-sided deck.

Steps: Install the edging. To trim out a step, begin as you would with a deck by installing a piece of perimeter edging, as shown in the top photo. Here again, you can get the trim to wrap around a corner by first cutting a 90-degree notch in the top edge (as shown on page 92) before screwing it to the stair tread.

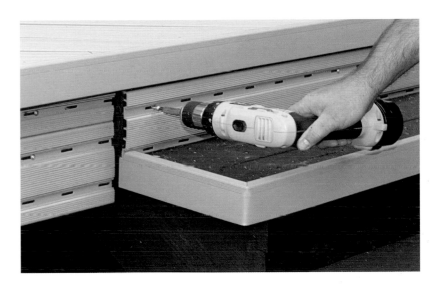

Steps: Cover the riser (optional). If desired, you can cover the riser with vinyl planking. Simply measure and cut a piece to length and width. Secure the plank to the risers as shown in the middle photo. Finish them off by covering the screws with a cover strip. If you don't want any of the

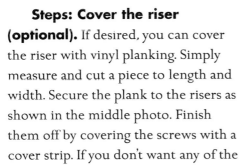

old deck to show, you can even cover the sides of the risers with deck planks. This will most likely take a bit of fancy cutting, but you'll end up with a no-maintenance surface. Alternatively, consider painting the sides to match the deck planking. Since these surfaces are vertical, they'll require much less attention over time compared to any horizontal surfaces, which are exposed to the elements.

Steps: Install the treads. With the edging in place, measure and cut planks to length and width as needed to cover the tread as you would for the fascia (see page 94). Secure the planks to the stair treads with pairs of screws every 9", as shown in the bottom photo.

Composite Decking

Anyone who's ever had a wood deck for more than a couple of years knows that they require maintenance. You've got to patrol the surface for nails that pop up annually. Every year or every other year, you need to apply a fresh coat of finish to help protect the wood and to keep it looking good. What if you didn't have to do this? And what if there were never any issues about splinters? If it sounds like a miracle, it practically is: composite decking. This stuff really is as good as it sounds.

For example, the TimberTech decking (www.timbertech.com) we used here to make over our high-end deck goes down fast and easy with no exposed fasteners, and requires no maintenance. None. Hard to believe, but it's true. Some manufacturers offer railing systems out of the same material—usually a mixture of wood chips or dust and plastic—so once the deck and railing are

installed, your only task is to enjoy it year after year.

Install starter strip. The installation of composite decking will depend on the type you're using. Solid composites go down much like solid wood. Extruded structural composites (like the TimberTech decking shown here) require a specific sequence. Tongue-and-groove products usually have a "starter strip"—a narrow piece with a groove to accept the first board. Since you'll probably need to rip a final board to width, it's best to place this against the house so that it will be less visible. With this in mind, install the starter strip on the rim joist and work back toward the house (middle photo).

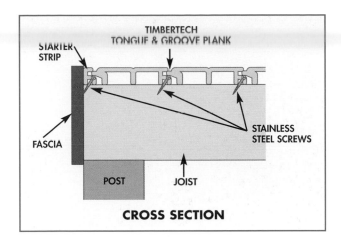

STARTER STRIP

TIMBERTECH TONGUE & GROOVE PLANK

FASCIA

STAINLESS STEEL SCREWS

POST

JOIST

CROSS SECTION

TimberTech system. TimberTech is an extruded composite in the form of tongue-and-groove planking (see the drawing above). An extrusion like this offers a number of excellent advantages over solid composite decking. First, as with any tongue-and-groove product, the fasteners are hidden—no nail "pops" or protruding screws to catch a bare foot. Second, with support "braces" engineered into the planks, the end result is a dimensionally stable and lightweight deck board that will stand up extremely well over time.

Mark around posts. In most cases you'll need to install planks to fit around the posts of your handrails. Here's how to locate the notches in the planks. Start by temporarily butting a plank up against the post, as shown in the bottom left photo. Then use a combination square and a pencil to

transfer the post location onto the plank as shown. Next, measure $^3/16$" out from this marked line—away from the post—to create a gap for clearance. Butt the plank up against the adjacent side of the post, and use the combination square to mark the other side of the notch.

Cut notch for post.
Once you've located the notch, you can cut it out. TimberTech is easy to cut with just about any saw. You can use a saber saw, a reciprocating saw, or just a handsaw, as shown in the photo at right. Because the cut is a stopped cut, a circular saw can be used to make only a partial cut; then you'll need to finish up the cut with a handsaw.

Attach to joists. Once the starter strip is in place, you can begin installing the planks. Since many composites are fragile until installed, always carry them on edge with at least two people to support each end. Use hand pressure only to slip the tongue of each plank into the groove. Drive a $2^1/2$" stainless steel screw through the lip below the groove at an angle into the joist, as shown in the bottom right photo. For best results, start fastening in the middle of the plank and work out toward the ends. Leave a $^3/16$" gap between boards laid end to end and between fascia boards and planks.

Continue and stagger.
After you've completed the first row of planks, begin on the second row, taking care to stagger the joints so the ends of the planks don't end up on the same joist, as shown in the top photo. Many manufacturers suggest staggering joints in thirds—that is, use a full-length plank for the first row, a two-thirds-length plank to start the second row, and a one-thirds-length plank to start the third row; repeat this pattern as needed. Also, just as you would when installing any deck board, it's best to allow the deck boards to "run wild" instead of trying to align them with the rim joists. To trim them to length, consult your plans for the desired overhang (if any) and measure and mark the cut by snapping a chalk line. Use a circular saw to carefully trim off the excess, making sure to cut on the waste side of the line.

Cut final plank to width. When you've got all the full-width planks installed, you'll likely need to cut the final piece to width to get it to fit in the remaining space between the last full plank and the house. Carefully measure, mark, and cut this piece to width, making sure to leave a 3/16" gap between the plank and the house, as shown in the middle photo.

Add a support block if necessary. To fully support the final plank, you may need to install a cleat or support under the unsupported end, as shown in the bottom photo. Consult the installation instructions for specifics on size and location of this support block.

Install the final plank. Since you won't have clearance to drive the screws for the final plank in at an angle, this last piece is screwed through its face into the ledger, as shown in the top photo. Note: Although it's not required, TimberTech can be finished with a high-quality oil-based paint or solid-color stain. If left untreated, it will weather to a natural driftwood gray. End caps and fascia boards are available to cover the exposed ends of the planks.

TRIMMING THE DECK

■ Unlike solid composites, which leave a clean edge when cut, an extruded structural composite leaves an edge that needs to be covered for best appearance. One way to handle this is to install fascia. Fascia is trim applied around the perimeter of a deck to the rim joists. If the deck boards were cut flush with the rim joists, the fascia is installed so the top edge is flush with the top of the deck boards. This type of trim is sometimes referred to as "picture frame," as the trim frames the decking. It's a good idea when installing fascia this way to leave a gap between the ends of the deck planks and the fascia for drainage and for wood movement.

Cut to size. The first step in installing fascia is to cut it to length. Use the longest planks possible—this cuts down on the number of joints. When you do need to join pieces together, use a scarf joint. Next, trim the fascia planks to width if necessary, as shown in the photo above. For the cleanest possible appearance, it's best to join the fascia at the corners with miters. If you notice any gaps after the fascia is installed, you can "burnish" the miter closed by rubbing the round shank of a screwdriver over the ends of the miter joint.

Attach to rim joists. The cleanest method of securing fascia to the rim joists is also the most work; it involves screwing the fascia to the rim joist from behind. The next cleanest method is to attach it with galvanized casing or finish nails (although this is the least secure method). If you choose instead to attach the fascia from the front with screws (as shown in the photo above), consider using stainless steel trim-head screws to minimize the appearance of the screws.

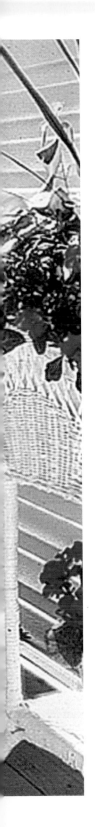

5

PORCHES

The porch is one of the first things people notice about your house. This first impression can be a warm, friendly greeting that invites visitors to stop and say "howdy," or it can be a stark, cold place that says "go away." Because porches have been slowly replaced by decks over the years, many homeowners tend to neglect their porches' appearance. That's too bad, because sometimes all it takes to change a porch into a pleasant, welcoming place is a weekend makeover. Often, the job isn't complicated, but just takes something as simple as a fresh coat of paint to the walls or trim, and maybe a new railing. What does your porch say about your home? If the answer is "not much," then you can change that fairly easily with any of the projects in this chapter.

Painting Exterior Walls

There's no quicker way to give a porch a makeover than to paint the exterior walls. An advantage that porch walls have over other exterior walls is that they are partially protected from the elements by the overhanging roof. (Naturally, this doesn't apply if your porch consists of just some steps, with little or no overhang.) Although you might be tempted to just slap on paint quickly, it's important not to skip any of the much-needed preparation steps for exterior paint. That's because any exterior wall exposed to moisture plus freeze/thaw cycles must have a continuous layer of paint (i.e., no holes, no gaps). This keeps moisture from sneaking in and breaking the bond between the wall and paint as the water freezes and thaws. Make sure to follow the preparation guidelines below and use a quality exterior latex wall paint.

Prepare the walls. The first step in getting a good paint bond is to clean the walls thoroughly. Scrub the walls lightly with a sponge or brush saturated with a cleaning solution of tri-sodium phosphate (TSP) to quickly strip off dirt and grime. Be sure to rinse the wall completely with clean water when done. Then take the time to patch holes and scrape off any loose paint. Feather-sand the areas where paint has been scraped off, using 120-grit open-coat sandpaper. Then place painter's cloths or drop cloths on the porch floor to catch drips and spills. Finally, fill in around trim with a high-quality paintable latex caulk, as shown in the bottom left photo.

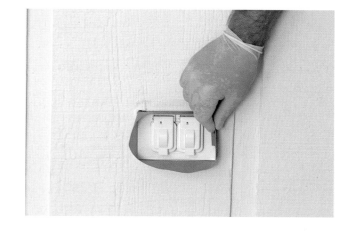

Mask if needed. Depending on your porch, you may or may not need to mask around obstacles. You may need to mask around window and door trim, or outdoor receptacles like the one shown in the middle photo. Painter's masking tape works best for this: It has less tendency to harm the underlying surface, as many other tapes can.

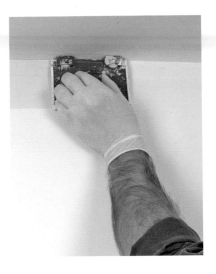

Paint the top perimeter. If you're covering a dark surface with a lighter paint, you may want to apply a coat of primer first. In addition to hiding the old color, priming also helps ensure a good bond between the old surface and the new paint. It's formulated to make the old surface more "receptive" to the paint. Priming also seals damaged areas and hides stains. And if you have the primer tinted to match the paint, you may need only one coat of finish paint. After the walls have been primed (if needed) and allowed to dry, the next step is to paint around the perimeter of the porch. A trim pad with rollers is a quick and efficient way to do this, as shown in the top left photo. The only trick to working with a trim pad is to keep the rollers free of paint. Check the rollers each time you load the pad, and remove any paint with a clean cloth.

Paint around the trim. There are a couple of tools you can use to paint around trim and obstacles. If you'll be painting the trim a different color (or using a different paint), you can make quick work of painting the adjacent walls

with a small roller, as shown in the bottom left photo. This small roller will paint right up to the trim. Be aware, though, that the roller is likely to get paint on the trim as well—that's why it's best used if you'll be painting the trim later. If you won't be painting trim, use the pad shown in the top left photo to paint the walls around the trim. The built-in rollers will keep the wall paint off the trim.

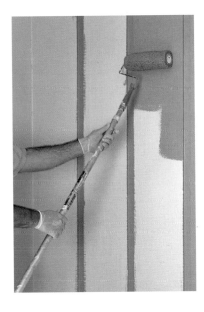

Paint the large surfaces. All that's left is to fill in the large spaces with paint as shown in the middle photo. A standard roller fitted with a disposable sleeve makes quick work of this. After you've rolled paint on a wall to cover it completely, go back and do what's called "striking off." Take your roller and begin at the top of the wall, and roll it all the way to the bottom in a continuous stroke. This will remove any roller marks and leave you with a smooth, clean wall. Apply a second coat if necessary.

Painting Trim

TOOLS

- Hammer
- Nail set
- Putty knife (optional)
- Caulking gun
- Sash or foam brush
- Trim pad or paint shield

The trim on a porch is like the accessories for an outfit of clothing. You can pick a color to match, accent, or contrast with the main color—in this case the porch walls, as shown in the top photo. As with porch walls, porch trim generally enjoys the protection of the roof and therefore will usually stay looking good longer than other exterior trim. The important thing is to prepare the trim properly for paint and then use a quality trim paint. Although water-based trim paints (like latex) are easier to clean up than oil-based paints, we've found that the oil-based versions stand up to the elements better over time.

Set any nails. If you're painting newly installed trim (see pages 106–107), you'll need to hide the nails. If the trim is old it may also need this, as continued humidity changes coupled with freeze/thaw cycles can cause nail "pop," where nails are literally squeezed out of the wood so they protrude. Carefully inspect the trim and set any protruding nails below the surface of the trim with a nail set and hammer, as shown in the bottom left photo. In most cases, you'll want the head of the nail about 1/8" below the surface.

Fill any holes. Once you've set the nails, you can go around and fill in the holes with putty. Make sure to use a putty that's formulated for exterior use and that will dry hard. Many types of putty never harden and should not be used outdoors. Press the putty into a hole with your finger, as shown in the bottom right photo, or with a putty knife. Just be sure to overfill the hole slightly, as most types of putty will shrink as they dry.

Sand the trim smooth. When you've filled all the holes, allow the putty to dry completely—your best bet here is to wait overnight. If the putty isn't dry when you paint over it, any moisture remaining can be trapped

inside and cause problems: The nails can rust and eventually stain the paint. Since you overfilled the holes, the putty will likely stand proud of the trim surface and need to be sanded flush, as shown in the top left photo. Use an open-coat aluminum oxide paper for this—it has less tendency to clog than most sandpaper. Then fill in any gaps between the trim and the walls or jamb with a paintable latex caulk and let the caulk dry.

Paint the edges. Now the trim is ready for paint. As with exterior walls, if you're painting a light color over a dark color, you'll be better off priming the trim first so that you'll need only one coat of trim paint. Consider having the primer tinted to match your trim color, as this will also help ensure one-coat coverage. There are a number of trim-painting accessories available to help keep trim paint off the walls. One is a paint shield, as shown in the top right photo.

Simply press the edge of the shield against the trim and paint. The only trick to using a shield is to wipe off trim paint before moving it to the next location. Alternatively, you can use a trim pad like the one shown in the top left photo on page 103.

Paint the trim. Now that you've painted the edges of the trim, you can paint the face of the trim, as shown in the middle photo. A sash brush or foam brush works great for this. After you've painted a single trim piece, go back and take a full-length stroke with the brush to remove any brush marks. This is similar to the striking-off technique described on the bottom of page 103. Brush on a second coat if needed, and allow the paint to dry completely before operating any windows or doors.

Installing Trim

TOOLS

- Locking pliers (optional)
- Tape measure
- Combination square
- Hammer and nail set
- Driver/drill and bits
- Caulking gun
- Circular or hand saw
- Power miter saw (optional)

There are many ways to install trim for a window or door. In modern homes, the most common way to attach trim is the miter style shown here. It's often referred to as picture frame trim, since it resembles the frame of a picture. Miter-cut trim is more of a challenge to install, because the 45-degree miter cuts must be accurate for the frame parts to come together with no gaps. The advantage to this style trim is that no end grain is exposed—the wood grain appears to run continuously around the perimeter of the window.

There are almost as many varieties of trim (or casing, as it's often called) available as there are styles of windows to choose from—everything from plain, simple molding to high-profile fancy trim. What you choose is really a matter of taste. When buying trim, be aware that there are a number of grades available. Paint-grade trim is often made by gluing up short pieces of different woods that are finger-jointed to make long pieces. Since the woods vary wildly in color and appearance, this trim should be painted. Note: Some home centers and lumberyards sell

pre-primed trim—all you need do is brush on a top-coat. Stain-grade trim offers fewer variations in grain and color and so is designed to accept a stain nicely. As it costs more than paint-grade, make sure you buy it only if you're intending to stain the trim; otherwise, buy paint-grade.

Mark reveal on jamb. To install miter trim, start by marking the reveal on each jamb. A reveal is a slight offset between the trim and the jamb; it allows for easier installation and provides a shadow line for visual interest. The easiest way to mark this is to set the blade of a combination square so it protrudes $1/8$", place a pencil against the blade of the square, press the head of the square against the jamb, and run the square and pencil around the perimeter to mark the reveal, as shown in the bottom photo.

Cut and nail the trim.

Most trim carpenters will start with the vertical trim. Place a piece of trim in position so its inside edge is flush with the marked reveal. Then make marks at the top and bottom (if applicable) of the trim where the horizontal and vertical reveal lines meet. Once these are cut and installed, move on to the top and bottom trim pieces. Measure these by running a tape measure between the installed side pieces, and cut pieces to fit. Note: If your window isn't square, start long and sneak up on the cut, adjusting the saw angle as necessary. Attach the outside edge of the trim with 3" casing nails to the studs and header that surround the window, as shown in the top left photo. Secure the inside edge to the jamb with 1 1/2" finish nails.

Lock-nail the miters.

Because miter joints tend to open and close as the humidity changes, it's a good idea to "lock-nail" the miters as shown in the

top right photo. Simply drive a nail in through the top or side of the miter joint into the adjacent piece to lock the pieces together. Since you'll be nailing close to the edge, it's a good idea to drill a small pilot hole first to prevent the trim from splitting as the nail is driven in.

Caulk around the trim.

Once all the trim is in place, use a hammer and nail set to set all nails slightly (1/8") below the surface of the trim. Fill these holes with an exterior-grade putty and when dry, sand smooth. Then use a high-quality paintable latex caulk to fill in any gaps between the trim and the exterior wall, as shown in the middle photo. Likewise, caulk any gaps between the trim and the jamb. Smooth the caulk with a wet finger and when that's dry, paint the trim with a quality oil-based trim paint (see pages 104–105 for more on painting trim).

REUSING TRIM

■ If you're planning on reusing any of the wood trim from the wall or wall section, don't pound the nails out through the face of the molding. All this usually does is split the wood, which creates a larger hole to fill once the trim is in place. Instead, pull the nails out from behind with a pair of locking pliers, as shown in the photo. This will create only a small hole to fill.

A New Wood Railing

The porches on some older homes and many new homes consist of nothing more elaborate than a roof supported by a couple of columns and either a wood or a concrete floor. But a railing on a porch is like shutters on a window. It's not absolutely essential, but it makes the home look more finished. A railing also provides additional privacy, and can even improve safety by offering a handhold and by creating a boundary for small children and pets. The wood railing shown here consists of a simple 2×4 frame, a set of 2×2 balusters, and a 1×6 cap rail.

Lay out the balusters. To make a wood railing to fit between a pair of columns, start by measuring the distance between the columns and cutting a pair of top/bottom rails to this measurement. Then lay the rails side by side with the ends flush and lay

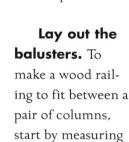

out the desired baluster spacing. First, subtract 3" from the length of the rails. Divide this number by 5 and round up to the next highest number. This is the number of spaces you'll have between the columns (C). Now divide B by C to determine baluster spacing. This number should not exceed 5". Mark a centerline on both rails and lay out the balusters, working from the center out toward the ends, as shown in the bottom left photo.

Assemble the frame. Before you can assemble the frame, you'll need to cut the end pieces to fit between the rails. How long these are will depend on the length of your balusters and how far you want the balusters to protrude past the bottom rail. Once you've decided on the length, cut the ends to length. Then assemble the frame by driving in pairs of galvanized deck screws through the rails and into the ends, as shown in the bottom right photo. Since you'll be driving these screws in near the ends of the rails, it's best to first drill pilot holes. Now you can attach the balusters. Align each baluster with the lines you laid out earlier and attach them with 2¹/₂" galvanized screws, as shown in the inset photo. Again, it's best to drill pilot holes first.

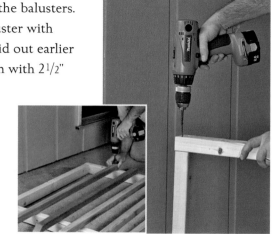

Attach railing to the columns. With the balusters in place, you can attach the assembled railing to the porch columns. Gently press the railing in place at the desired distance up from the porch floor. Then use a level to make sure the top is level before screwing through the ends of the frame and into the columns, as shown in the top photo. Use 2 1/2" or 3" galvanized deck screws for this, spacing them out every 12" or so.

Add the cap rail. Although you could leave the railing as it is, you'd leave the frame assembly screws exposed. Not only would this be unattractive, but it would also cause problems over time— moisture would wick along the screw threads and encourage rust to develop. A nice finishing touch is

to add a 1×6 cap rail. Measure the distance from column to column and cut a cap to fit. If you have access to a router, consider easing the top edges by routing a 1/4" or 3/8" round-over. Secure the cap rail to the frame assembly by screwing up through the frame with 2" galvanized screws. If your drill won't fit between the balusters, secure the cap rail from above but drive the screw below the surface of the cap (as shown in the bottom left photo). Then fill this hole with exterior-grade putty.

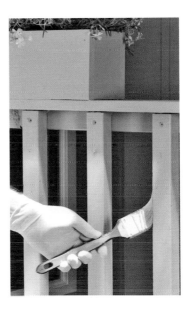

Paint the railing if desired. To protect your new porch railing, you should apply some type of finish. If you used dissimilar woods (as we did here), it's best to paint the railing for a uniform color, as shown in the middle photo. Alternatively, you can apply an exterior stain, clear finish, or water-proofing finish.

Composite Railing

TOOLS

- Circular or miter saw
- Tape measure
- Try or combination square
- Electric drill and bits
- Screwdriver

If you want to add a railing to your porch, but you're not interested in annual maintenance (scraping and painting or staining), consider a composite railing. The system shown here is manufactured by TimberTech (www.timbertech.com). Once installed it doesn't require any maintenance—ever. The TimberTech railing system consists of a set of identical top and bottom rails that are spanned by balusters. The top rail is covered with a rail cap and the railing attaches to balusters secured to the porch columns.

Install the end balusters. To begin installing a composite railing system, start by attaching a baluster to each inside porch column (or exterior wall section, as shown in the bottom left photo). Take care to posi-

tion the baluster to leave the desired space beneath the bottom rail; check with your local building inspector to determine the maximum allowable space. An easy way to position the baluster is to set it on a rail section that's level and is resting on a spacer block (in our case, a brick). Then center the baluster and screw it to the column or wall with 3" galvanized deck screws.

Lay out the balusters on the rails. Just as we did with the wood railing shown on pages 108–109, we'll install the balusters on the top and bottom rails before securing the assembled railing to the porch columns or walls. To do this, you'll need to first locate the baluster positions. With the TimberTech system, first measure the distance between two posts (A). Then subtract 1.35" to get the distance between the columns from the center of the column-mounted balusters (B). Divide this number by 5 and round up to the next highest number. This is the number of spaces you'll have between the posts (C). Now divide B by C to determine baluster spacing. This number should not exceed 5". After you've determined baluster spacing, cut two pieces of top/bottom rail to fit between the posts. Then mark a centerline on both rails and lay out the balusters. Work from the center out toward the ends, as shown in the bottom right photo.

Attach the balusters to the rails. To attach the balusters, first drill pilot holes for the screws at each baluster location in both rails. Then, working on one rail at a time, drive a screw up through the rail and into the baluster. Take care to hold the baluster firmly in place as you drive in the screw, as shown in the top photo. When you have all the balusters attached to one rail, attach the opposite rail to the balusters, making sure the rail fronts are facing in the same direction.

Attach the railing to the end balusters. Once a rail section has been assembled, you can attach it to the columns. Just slip the ends of the top/bottom rails over the balusters

mounted to the columns or walls (a helper makes this a lot easier), as shown in the bottom inset photo. Then secure the rail assembly to the column or wall balusters by driving a screw through each rail end into the balusters, as shown in the bottom left photo. Repeat for any remaining sections.

Attach the rail cap. All that's left to complete the composite railing is to add the rail cap. Measure the distance between the columns or walls and cut a piece of cap rail to length. Then set it on top of the top rail so the groove in its bottom aligns with the long tenon on top of the top rail. Secure the cap rail to the top rail by driving screws up through the top rail and into the cap rail, as shown in the middle photo.

Adding Ornamentation

TOOLS

• Caulking gun
• Hammer
• Nail set
• Putty knife (optional)

To add visual interest (and maybe a touch of whimsy) to a porch, consider ornamentation. This can be anything from simple trim molding to fancy decorative scrollwork, as shown here. Although the scrollwork we used here looks like wood, it's actually urethane foam sculpted to resemble wood. Urethane millwork like this has numerous advantages. First, since it's made of foam, it's very light. This makes it easy to install and also less affected by gravity, which tends to cause wood scrollwork to sag over time. Second, because it's not wood, it won't expand and contract as the seasons change. As a non-moving material, it won't tend to loosen its fasteners, nor will it loosen the paint on its surface. The urethane scrollwork shown here is manufactured by Fypon (www.fypon.com) and comes in a huge variety of shapes, sizes, and designs.

Mark the position. The first step to installing urethane ornamentation is to locate and mark its desired location. A helper is useful for this, as it's hard to determine the visual impact of mold-

ing when you're right next to it. Place the scrollwork where you think it should go, and have someone look at the house from the sidewalk or street. Adjust as needed and when you've located the perfect spot, use a pencil to mark its location on the house, as shown in the top right photo.

Paint the scrollwork if desired. Urethane foam takes paint readily, so if you'd like to add some color, it's a lot easier to paint it now before it's installed. For intricate ornamentation like the scrollwork shown in the bottom photo, spray-on paint works best. Make sure to select a spray paint that's rated for exterior use. Since these surfaces will be exposed to the elements, it's best to apply two coats.

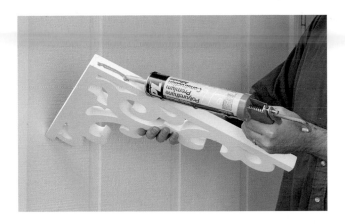

Apply an adhesive. Foam scrollwork should never be installed with just fasteners. It's designed to be installed with both fasteners and a bead of high-quality, urethane-based adhesive. You don't need a lot here: About a 1/8" bead on both mating surfaces will work fine. You'll find that this combination of adhesive and fasteners along with the foam's built-in flexibility will make installing scrollwork a snap.

Set the scroll-work in place.
To install ornamentation once the adhesive has been applied, simply press it in place, taking care to align its edges with the pencil marks you made earlier (top right photo). Hold the piece in place for a couple of minutes and, if necessary, apply a couple of strips of tape to keep it in place until the adhesive sets up.

Secure with nails. All that's left is to secure the ornamentation with nails as shown in the bottom photo. Make sure to use hot-dipped galvanized nails or another exterior-rated nail. Also, since foam dents easily, stop driving the nail when it's 1/8" or so away from the surface. Then finish the job with a nail set and a hammer. When you've installed all the nails and set them, go back and fill in any holes with an exterior-rated putty. If you painted the scrollwork, touch up the putty spots with the same paint.

6

PATIOS

Webster's defines a patio as a "recreation area that adjoins a dwelling, is often paved, and is adapted especially for outdoor dining." Webster, though, couldn't foresee most modern patios. In many cases a patio is no more than a slab of concrete attached to the back of a house; hardly a "recreation area," but the potential is there. One of the best ways to turn a concrete slab into a lovely space for outdoor dining is to cover it. This can range from a simple corrugated roof to an elaborate arbor. For a deluxe makeover that will turn your patio into real living space, consider adding a sunroom—the most challenging yet most rewarding project in this chapter. Additionally, you can paint the concrete or tile it (see chapter 4) and add railings or planters (see chapter 9). Why not start this weekend to convert your slab into a real recreation area?

A Corrugated Roof

A covered patio is one of life's simple pleasures. But, covering a patio with a conventional shingle roof can take a lot of money, time, and hard work. If you're looking for a basic, sheltering cover that blocks wind and rain, consider building a simple frame to support corrugated plastic roofing. Although not designed to handle heavy snow loads, a corrugated roof can stand up quite well to winter if the pitch is sufficient (around 1-in-12), and if suitable framing and blocking is installed.

A corrugated roof can stand alone but is generally more stable if one side is attached to your house (see the drawing on the opposite page). In years past, it was quite a challenge to attach the wavy plastic to flat framing without breaking the panels. Savvy roofing manufacturers now produce special closure strips that make assembly quick and easy. These strips are basically pieces of plastic that

are flat on one face and wavy on the other to match the panels. The Suntuf system used here is manufactured by Palram Americas (www.suntuf.com).

Install the posts. To install a corrugated roof, the first step is to build a frame to support the panels. The frame consists of a beam supported by vertical posts. Rafters then span the space between the home's fascia and the beam. Blocking is added to support the panels (see the drawing on the opposite page). The first frame parts to install are the posts. Consult your local building code for size and spacing specifications. The posts attach to the patio via a set of post anchors bolted to the concrete pad (inset). Then you cut the posts to length to create the desired pitch and attach them to the anchors (take care to make sure they're plumb, as shown in the bottom photo).

patio and rest on the beam are attached to the fascia via a set of joist hangers. Joist spacing will vary between 12" and 24", depending on your local building code. After you've identified the spacing, use a tape measure to mark the joist locations on the fascia as shown in the bottom photo; transfer these measurements to the beam as well. Then install a joist hanger at each location, taking care to align the bottom edges of the hangers with the bottom edge of the fascia, as shown in the photo above.

Attach the beam. Now you can cut the beam to length (here again, see your local building code for size and length), and secure it to the vertical posts with framing connectors, as shown in the top left photo. Then cut a set of braces for each post and install them as shown in the inset photo.

Install the joist hangers. Once the beam is in place, you can begin work on the opposite side—the fascia of the house. The rafters that span the

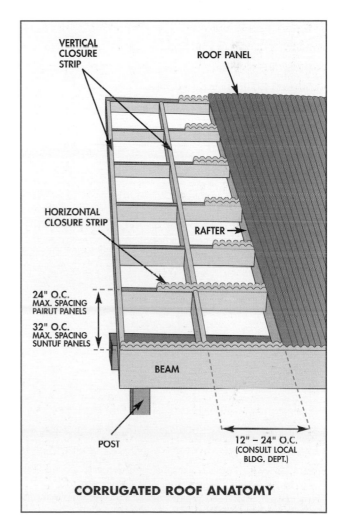

VERTICAL CLOSURE STRIP

ROOF PANEL

HORIZONTAL CLOSURE STRIP

RAFTER

24" O.C. MAX. SPACING PAIRUT PANELS

32" O.C. MAX. SPACING SUNTUF PANELS

BEAM

POST

12" – 24" O.C. (CONSULT LOCAL BLDG. DEPT.)

CORRUGATED ROOF ANATOMY

Prepare the rafters.

Now you're ready for the rafters. Before these can be installed, there are a couple of things to do. The first thing is to lay out the location of the blocking. This is typically 24" on center. Use a framing square to transfer the locations to each rafter, as shown in the top left photo. Next, place a rafter in a joist hanger and set the other end on the beam. Mark the fascia end to match the pitch of the roof, using a small level, and then mark the same angle on the opposite end (with the desired overhang), using the level as shown in the inset photo above.

Attach rafters to the beam. Now you can secure the other ends of the rafters. Start by aligning the end rafter with the location marks you made earlier on the beam. Then use a 3-4-5 triangle to make sure this rafter is perpendicular to the fascia. To do this, measure out 3' on the rafter and make a mark. Then measure out 4' along the fascia and make a mark. Now measure between the two marks. If the rafter is perpendicular to the fascia, this measurement will be exactly 5'. If it's not, the pieces aren't perpendicular and the rafter position will have to be adjusted. Once you've got the first rafter aligned, you can use its position to make sure the remaining rafters are installed correctly. Secure each rafter to the beam with the framing connector, shown in the top right photo.

Attach the roof fascia. With all the rafters installed, the last framing task is to cut and install the fascia (if applicable). If your rafters extend out over the beam, you should install a fascia board to help prevent the rafters from moving about due to wind, rain, and humidity variations. Just measure from one end of the rafter to the other and cut a fascia to length.

Attach rafters to the fascia. Cut the angles you just marked on the ends of all the rafters and then begin installing them. Place a rafter in the joist hanger and attach it to the fascia by driving in a set of galvanized nails through the joist hanger, through the rafter, and into the fascia, as shown in the bottom left photo. Make sure to use a nail at each nailing flange location.

Attach it to the ends of the rafters with galvanized nails, as shown in the bottom right photo.

Add the blocking. To fully support the plastic corrugated panels, blocking is added between the rafters every 24" on center. Working on one section at a time, measure and cut lengths of 2-by material to fit between the rafters. Align the blocking with the location marks you made earlier on the rafters, and secure each piece of blocking with galvanized nails, as shown in the top photo. One end of each blocking piece can be face-nailed, while the opposite end will need to be toenailed. If you have access to a framing nailer (rent one at most home and rental centers), it will make quick work of this tedious job.

Attach closure strips to blocking. Now that the framing is complete, go ahead and start installing the closure strips to the blocking. Start at one end of the roof and position the first piece so its end aligns with the end of the blocking. Secure the closure strip to the blocking with nails or screws (screws tend to hold better, and there's less risk of damaging the closure strips), as shown in the middle photo. The Suntuf strips are designed with snap-together ends to ensure perfect alignment. Continue snapping together strips and securing them to the blocking until you reach the other end; cut the final strip to length if needed. Repeat for the remaining rows of blocking.

Attach the vertical closure strips. To support the sides of the panels, vertical closure strips are attached to the rafters as shown in the bottom photo. Start on the end rafters and run strips the full length of the rafter. Then install strips on the rafters to fit between the ribbed closure strips you installed earlier.

Install the panels. Now you can install the actual corrugated panels. Because you'll need to reach over the panels to fasten them to the framing, it's best to work from the center of the framing out toward the ends, as shown in the top left photo. Just as with any other roofing product, if you're installing overlapping panels (or shingles), you always start at the end away from the peak or ridge (in this case, the house fascia) and work toward it. So position the first center panel so its end is flush with the end fascia that overhangs the beam.

Drill holes for the fasteners. The panels are fastened to the roof framing with special corrugated fasteners (see the sidebar below). The fasteners fit through holes that you drill in the panels. Suntuf recommends using a $3/16"$ drill bit. This creates a slightly oversized hole that accommodates thermal movement that could make the panels buckle. Drill at the peak of each corrugated wave, through the closure strip, and into the framing, as shown in the top right photo. Suntuf recommends spacing fasteners every other rib.

CORRUGATED ROOFING FASTENERS

■ Although you could install plastic corrugated roofing with standard screws, don't. Most roofing manufacturers sell special fasteners designed for their panels. In addition to being galvanized, these screws have an EPDM washer—a tough, flexible rubber washer that will create a watertight seal around the hole once the screw is installed. Suntuf makes screws for driving into sheet metal or wood.

Work out toward ends. Once you've got the holes drilled, you can begin installing the fasteners (top photo). These fasteners have hex heads, so it's easy to drive them in with a magnetic nut-driver fitted into a driver drill. Work from the center out. After you've tightened each screw, reverse the drill and back the screw out one-half turn to keep from compressing the washer too much—it should just touch the panel and not be squished. Install the remaining panels that are flush with the overhanging end of the framing.

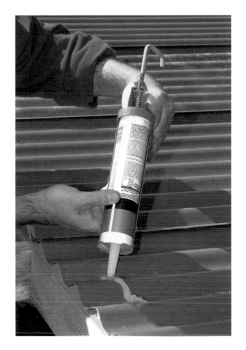

Apply sealant to the seams. Depending on the length of your patio roof, you may need to install additional panels. These will lie on top of the existing panels. To get a watertight seal between the overlapping ends, apply a generous bead of silicone caulk to the bottom panel, as shown in the middle photo. This stuff tends to be messy, so work on one panel at a time.

Overlap the panels. Now install the remaining panels (bottom photo). If necessary, measure and cut them to length. The panels cut easily with a circular saw fitted with a plywood blade installed backwards, or a utility knife and a straightedge. Cut these panels to length to allow for a 4" overlap at the seams, and install them as you would the other panels. Most manufacturers also sell plastic flashing to handle the transition between the existing roof or wall and the new corrugated roof. Install this if needed.

Building an Arbor

Although a patio arbor does provide some relief from the sun, it's mainly decorative. There are two basic structural choices when adding an arbor to a patio: freestanding or attached to the house. Since a freestanding structure must support all of the weight of the unit, it usually consists of large beams, often with cross braces to prevent racking. Units that are attached to the house (like the one shown here) require only half the support structure, since half of the weight is borne by the house. How much sun comes through the arbor will depend on the material you use on top and its spacing. Lattice, 2-by, and 1-by material are all popular and appropriate. Alternatively, there is screening available that can filter out the sun's rays somewhat.

Set metal anchors in the pad. The first step to building an arbor is to locate the posts that will support the overhead frame. The size and location of the posts will be defined by your local codes. The best method for attaching the posts to a con-

crete pad is to use an adjustable post base like the one shown in the photo at right. This type of connector raises the post up off the pad and keeps water from wicking up the post and eventually causing rot or decay. Your best bet for drilling holes for concrete anchors is a hammer drill, fitted with a masonry bit. If you don't own one of these, rent one from a home or rental center. Before tightening the anchors completely, butt a long, straight 2×4 up against the outside faces of the post base to ensure that they all line up.

Prefinish all the parts. If you're planning to apply a finish to your arbor, you'll find that it's a lot easier to apply the finish before assembling the project. Not only is it easier to reach parts when they're not overhead, but prefinishing also ensures that all surfaces of the parts will be protected—something that's highly unlikely if you were to finish the arbor after it's assembled. Brush on one or two coats of the finish of your choice, as shown in the top left photo.

Install the posts. After all the arbor parts have dried completely, the next step is to start assembly. Begin by inserting a post in each post base, making sure it's plumb, and then fasten it to

the post base with galvanized joist-hanger nails, as shown in the top right photo. Now you can attach post caps to the tops of the posts to accept the beam that spans them. These just slip over the ends and are secured with galvanized joist-hanger nails. Note: Before you slip the cap on, it's a good idea to brush on an extra coat of finish to the top of the post. Flat surfaces like this, even when covered, tend to collect moisture and are prone to rot and insect damage.

Install the beam(s). With the posts and post caps installed, you can add the beam (or beams, if making a freestanding arbor). Measure, mark, and cut the beam(s) to length to span the posts. Here again, the size and length of the beams will be defined by local codes. You can install the beams flush with the tops of the posts, or allow them to overhang a bit for added visual interest. Have a helper for lifting each beam into place and holding the beam steady until you can secure it with galvanized joist nails, as shown in the bottom photo.

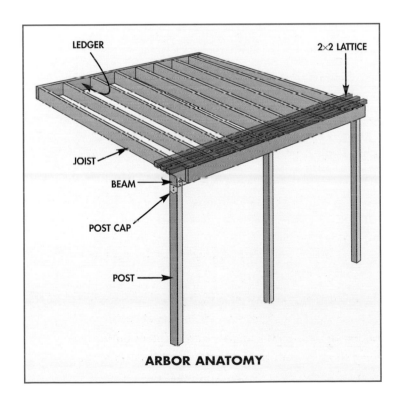

LEDGER

2×2 LATTICE

JOIST

BEAM

POST CAP

POST

ARBOR ANATOMY

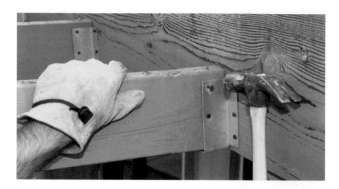

Add the bracing. To prevent the arbor from racking, it's a good idea to install braces between the posts and the beams. These can be nothing more than lengths of 2×4 or 4×4 mitered at a 45-degree angle at each end. Secure the braces to the posts and beam with galvanized deck screws, as shown in the top left photo. Make sure to check with a framing square that the post is perpendicular to the beam before you attach both ends of the brace.

Install the joists. With the post and beam unit(s) assembled, the next step is to span them with joists. For a free-standing arbor, these can be toe-nailed to the beams or attached with hurricane ties, as shown in the inset photo. If you're building an attached arbor, one end of the joists will attach to the house and the other will rest on the beam. To attach joists to the house, first lay out their positions on the fascia; the distance between the joists will be determined by your local code. Once you've got the joists laid out, attach a joist hanger at each joist location. Then set a joist in the hanger and secure it with galvanized nails, as shown in the top right photo. Secure the other end to the beam with a hurricane tie (inset).

Add blocking if desired. To prevent the joists from bowing over time, consider adding blocking between the joists. These are just lengths of 2×4 cut to fit between the joists and are positioned every 24" or so on center. They are secured with nails, as shown in the bottom photo.

Add rim joists. Depending on the look you're after, you may or may not wish to add rim joists. Rim joists cover the exposed ends of the joists and not only look better, but they also help prevent the joists from bowing or moving out of position over time. To install a rim joist, measure from one end joist to the opposite end and cut a 2×4 or 2×6 to length. Attach the rim joist to the ends of the rafter with galvanized nails or screws, as shown in the top photo.

Add slats to top of joists. At this point, you can add the fill to the top of the rafters. There are many choices for fill (lattice, 1-by, and 2-by material), and how you install it will depend on the type. If you're using individual boards (like the 2×2's shown in the middle photo), start at one end and nail or screw the board to the joist. Then use a scrapwood spacer to align the next board and fasten it in place. Repeat until the rafters are covered. (Since lattice is pre-assembled, it goes on a lot quicker—just make sure to support it periodically with cross supports or blocking to prevent it from bowing.)

Secure the arbor to the house if possible. In cases where you've installed a freestanding arbor and it's close to your house, consider adding an extra bit of support by attaching it to the fascia or wall of your home, as shown in the bottom photo. Simple 2×4 cleats, cut to span between the two and secured with galvanized screws, will help prevent the arbor from racking under high winds or heavy snow loads.

Adding a Sunroom

TOOLS

- Tape measure and framing square
- Level and hammer
- Circular saw or power miter saw
- Hammer drill (optional)
- Driver/drill and bits
- Socket set and nut-drivers
- Utility knife or scissors
- Caulking gun

We think the ultimate makeover for a patio is installing a sunroom. A sunroom adds living space to your home by making your patio usable three or even four seasons of the year. A quality sunroom should shed water, bring in as much natural light as possible, allow in breezes during warm weather, and protect you in cold weather. That's exactly what the sunroom we chose to install in our high-end patio makeover does. It's manufactured by SunPorch Structures, Inc. (www.sunporch.com) and is the only sunroom we've found that's designed to be installed by a homeowner. (That's not to say you can't have one installed by a local contractor, if you prefer.)

A typical sunroom consists of a metal frame that accepts window and roof panels, and doors, if desired. The metal frame is made up of a base channel that accepts the end walls and the internal frame sections, as shown in the bottom drawing. Most are available with screens in the top windows or in both the top and bottom windows. Accessories include roof vents, pet doors, ceiling fans, etc.

Before you start planning on adding on a sunroom, check your local building codes. Code varies from state to state on these structures. Some states require special engineering, while others don't even require a permit as long as you're mounting the sunroom to an existing deck or patio and not altering what is shown on your lot plan. The one key to a successful installation is that the deck or patio you're mounting the sunroom to must be level. Since most decks and patios are slanted away from the house to promote water runoff, you'll likely need to cut and install long wedges under the base channels to make them level. If you need to do this, make sure to use pressure-treated wood that's rated for direct ground contact.

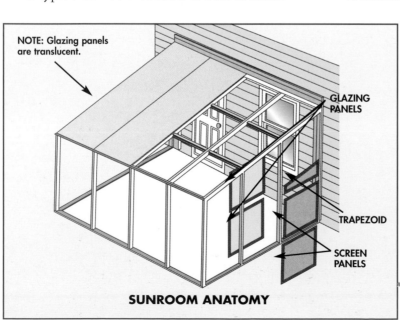

NOTE: Glazing panels are translucent.

GLAZING PANELS

TRAPEZOID

SCREEN PANELS

SUNROOM ANATOMY

Attach the channel parts. To build a sunroom, start by assembling the base channel that serves as the foundation. The base channel may be U-shaped (for most installations) or L-shaped (for end wall installations). Since all parts of the sunroom are shipped directly to you, you may have to connect a few pieces to create the long wall, as shown in the top photo. These pieces are held together via a set of splice brackets that are secured with screws (inset photo).

Connect the channel at the corners. If you're assembling a U-shaped base channel, the ends of the channel will be mitered. Use the corner brackets supplied to attach the long and short legs of the base channel, as shown in the middle photo. Here again, it's imperative that you make sure this channel rests level on the deck or patio before proceeding.

Attach the base to the deck or patio. Once you've installed pressure-treated wedges under the base channel (if necessary to level it), you can secure the base channel to the deck or patio. The type of fastener you use will depend on the surface you're mounting the base channel to. For concrete, use 1/4" × 3 1/2" lock bolts. On wood decks, use 1/4" × 2 1/2" lag screws. Install fasteners about every 3 feet, as shown in the bottom photo.

Attach the vertical mounting brackets.

With the base channel secured, your next step is to attach brackets to the base channel that accept the vertical columns. These brackets are screwed to the base channel, as shown in the top photo. There's no need to drill here because the holes for these brackets are pre-drilled at the factory. Since most of the screws and bolts in the SunPorch kit are hex-head, you'll find that a nut-driver mounted in a driver/drill will make quick work of this.

Install the header and the rafter brackets.

At this point you can start building the frame assemblies. There are two end assemblies (one if you're doing an end wall install), and a set of inner frames. Depending on the depth of your sunroom, you may need to first connect headers to rafters. Then you can attach the vertical columns, as shown in the middle photo. All of these parts are connected via a set of mounting brackets. Both these and the header, rafter, and column parts are predrilled. Assembly is quick and easy—it's sort of like a large-scale Erector Set.

Attach angled columns to end assemblies.

To complete the frame assemblies, you'll need to attach a set of angled columns to the end frames. These are angled gradually shorter from back to front, to match the pitch of the roof. Each angled column attaches to the header/rafter assembly by way of a mounting bracket, as shown in the bottom photo.

Attach end assembly to base channel. Now the fun begins: It's time to start erecting the frame. Start by installing one of the end assemblies. With the aid of a helper, lift the assembly up and place the bottoms of the vertical columns over the brackets you installed earlier on the base channel. While the helper holds the assembly in place, you can secure the end assembly to the base channel by driving screws through the vertical columns and into the base channel brackets, as shown in the top photo.

Attach end assembly to ledger. With the bottom of the end assembly secure, you can attach the top to the house. The header will have a header bracket installed that will butt up against the fascia, ledger, or wall, as shown in the middle photo. Take the time to make sure the vertical column is plumb before marking and drilling holes in the fascia, ledger, or wall. Secure the header with the fasteners recommended by the manufacturer.

Add roof supports. Now that you've got a starting point for the sunroom frame, you can begin to add the remaining sections. Each section is spanned by a set of horizontal roof supports. You'll need to install a set of these, add the next frame section, and repeat until the entire frame is erected. Attach the horizontal roof supports to the brackets installed on the header/rafter assemblies, as shown in the bottom photo.

Install the next frame assembly. With one set of roof supports installed, lift up and position the adjacent frame assembly, as shown in the top left photo. Secure this assembly to the bracket in the base channel, to the fascia, ledger, or wall (making sure it's plumb), and to the horizontal roof supports you just installed. Repeat this sequence for the other frame assemblies by first installing the horizontal roof supports and then adding the next frame assembly.

Secure opposite end assembly. When you've worked your way to the opposite end, finish off the frame by installing the opposite end assembly, as shown in the top right photo. Use the same routine here: Secure it to the base channel, then to the fascia, ledger, or wall, and then to the horizontal roof supports. Now it's starting to look like something.

UNDER-EAVE ASSEMBLIES

■ The folks at SunPorch realize that a sunroom can't always attach to an exterior wall on a home. In many cases, it needs to attach to the overhanging fascia. But what about the space under the eaves? Not a problem. Just supply SunPorch with the measurements, and they'll custom-make a frame and set of panels to fill in this space.

Attach 2×4's to the exterior wall. The first step to filling in under an eave is to attach vertical 2×4's to the exterior wall. Make sure that they are plumb, and secure them with exterior-rated adhesive and lag screws.

Install the frame parts. Now you can install the frame parts. Just like the main frame, you'll have a section of base channel and a vertical column. Attach these according to the manufacturer's instructions.

Install the panels. All that's left is to install the panels. These are installed just like the other top and bottom panels described on page 135, except there are no screens on either panel.

Attach the top ridge. To create a seal between the frame and the fascia, wall, or ledger, a top ridge is added at the junction of these two parts, as shown in the top photo. Before placing and securing this ridge, make sure to follow the manufacturer's directions on caulking. They'll want you to apply a high-quality silicone caulk to the top back-side of the top ridge and to any header that it rests on.

Attach the header caps. The roof panels attach to the frame via a set of extruded strips called header caps. It's easy to get a watertight seal for your roof if—and only if—you religiously follow the manufacturer's caulking directions. Apply a bead of silicone under each header cap before securing it to a header with screws, as shown in the middle photo. Attach header caps to all the header/rafter assemblies.

Install the front eave. Before you can install the roof panels, there are a number of things to do. The first thing is to attach the front eave to the frame, as shown in the bottom photo. Here again, you'll want to follow the manufacturer's instructions on where to caulk before securing the front eave with screws. In most cases, the front eave will consist of two pieces butted up against each other.

Seal the panel ends. The roofing panels supplied by SunPorch will also need some attention before being installed. The ends of each panel are covered with tape, as shown in the top photo. The top end is covered with aluminum tape to keep dirt and moisture from entering the extruded channels. The bottom edge is covered with a spun vent adhesive tape that allows any condensed moisture to flow out of the channels and drain away.

Apply gasket to the battens. The roof panels are held in place by screwing battens down over each joint where the panels meet over a header/rafter assembly. The screws are driven into the header caps you installed earlier. To create a watertight seal, you apply self-adhesive foam to both underside edges of each batten, as shown in the middle photo.

Apply gasket to gasket strips. As added insurance against moisture problems, you'll also apply foam gasket to both sides of the header caps you installed earlier, as shown in the bottom photo. Take care not to stretch this foam as you apply it; this can create thin spots where moisture may sneak through.

Install the roof panels. OK, enough gasket fun. Now it's time to install the roof panels. Start at one end of the frame and apply silicone caulk as directed. Then with the aid of a helper, lift and position the roof panel in place, as shown in the top photo. The panel should fit comfortably between the top ridge and the front eave you installed earlier.

Secure the sides of the roof panels.

To secure the roof panel, start by placing a batten over the edge near the end assembly. Secure the batten with the special washered screws provided, as shown in the middle photo. These screws have a combination metal/neoprene washer that will create a seal around the hole in the batten as it's screwed down. (The opposite side of the panel won't get secured until you install the next roof panel.)

Secure the ends of the roof panels.

Now you can secure the ends of the roof panels. These are secured with a set of single battens that are quite different from the long battens used to secure the sides of the panels. The single battens fit into grooves in the top ridge and front eave and are secured with longer screws, as shown in the bottom photo. (See the assembly manual for detailed directions on caulking, gasketing, and mounting.)

Seal the panels. Once the single battens are in place, apply a generous bead of silicone caulk as directed in the assembly manual to the top ridge and front eave batten, as shown in the top photo. Although these battens do have gaskets, the added caulk will serve as extra protection against future leaks. Now you can move on to the next roof panel. Set it in place, and secure the far end with a batten. Screw down the ends with single battens, caulk, and move on until you reach the opposite end.

Install the end wall fillers. With the roof complete, you can turn your attention to the walls. Because the wall panels are square and the roof is pitched, you'll need to install a set of end fillers directly below the header/rafter assemblies on the end frame assemblies. These are either solid aluminum tapered wedges (as shown in the middle photo) or tapered wedges with clear plastic inserts. These are simply held in place and then secured with screws.

Install screens in panels. Before you can install the wall panels, there's some work to do. For any panel that comes with a screen, you'll need to install the screen lock hardware on the screen (bottom right photo). Then install the screen in the panel using this hardware to lock the screen in place, as shown in the bottom left photo. Do this for each wall unit that has a screen.

Install the lower panels.

Install the wall panels by first securing the lower panel and then adding the upper panel. A watertight seal is created by applying a putty-like gasket around the edges of the wall frame, as shown in the top left photo. Then the lower wall panel is positioned so it's centered between the vertical columns and secured with screws, as shown in the top right photo.

Install the upper panels.

To create a seal between the upper and lower panels, apply gasket to the top outside edge of the lower panel, as shown in the middle left photo. Then position the upper panel so that it's also centered between the vertical columns, and screw it in place (middle right photo). This sequence of applying gasket, installing the lower panel, more gasket, followed by the upper panel is repeated until all the wall panels are installed.

Install the door.

All that's left is to add a door or doors, as shown in the bottom photo. These go in similarly to the wall panels. Apply gaskets to the vertical columns and install the door frame pieces. Then add the door panels just like you did for the wall panels. Additional hardware to install includes the door lever and latch and the door closer.

7

FLOORS

Quick, what's the most abused floor of your home? Your kitchen, right? Nope. Bathroom? Not that, either. The floors that take the worst beating are your exterior floors: the ones on your deck, porch, or patio. Why? Because not only are they exposed to outdoor foot traffic with all its dirt and debris, but they're also exposed to the elements. This one-two punch is usually too much for most exterior floors, and so they often quickly age and end up looking tired and worn-out.

The good news, though, is that it's easy to give an exterior floor a makeover. You can start on a very modest scale with a simple cleaning and basic repair, and move all the way up to more extensive jobs, like installing colorful indoor/outdoor carpeting or hardworking, elegant tile. The secret to a successful outdoor floor is combining the right materials with the proper know-how.

Cleaning Concrete

TOOLS

- Garden sprayer
- Hose
- Stiff-bristle broom or brush

How easy or difficult it is to clean concrete will depend how stained it is. Concrete that's just dirty can be cleaned with regular household detergent. Stubborn grime can often be scrubbed off, but seriously blemished concrete requires an acid-based cleaner to remove tough stains.

Spray on cleaner. Regardless of the cleaner you're going to use, it's best to start by masking off any sensitive areas, such as adjacent walls and plants. Cover these with plastic sheathing and secure with tape, as shown in the inset photo below. Household detergent can be mixed in a bucket and poured directly on the slab. Chemical cleaners are best applied with a garden sprayer, as shown in the bottom left photo. Make sure to follow the manufacturer's mixing instructions and wear old clothes,

plastic gloves, and eye protection when working with these harsh chemicals. Keep pets and children away until you are finished.

Scrub concrete with brush. For stubborn stains, use a deck brush or stiff-bristle broom to scrub wetted areas as needed to lift the stains (photo at right). You may find it helpful to apply more cleanser or chemical cleaner as you scrub.

Rinse off cleaner. When the entire slab is clean, rinse off all cleaner with fresh water as shown in the bottom right photo. If you used a chemical cleaner, rinse the slab completely and then go back and rinse it again. Let the slab dry totally before allowing foot traffic.

Repairing Concrete

If part of your makeover involves concrete, odds are it'll be cracked in some places and in need of repair. If the cracks are less than 3/8" wide, you can fix them yourself with some concrete patch. Cracks larger than this are best left to a professional.

Widen and clean cracks. To repair cracked concrete, start by chipping away any loose areas. Wearing eye protection, use a hammer and cold chisel to gently clear away loose concrete on the

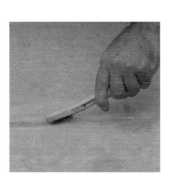

sides of the crack, as shown in the bottom left photo. Once you have the loose parts broken off, go back with a wire brush and clean out the crack as shown in the photo at left.

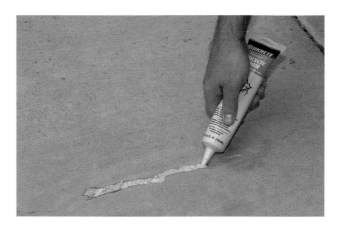

Apply patch compound. With the crack cleaned, the next step is to apply a concrete patch. These come in squeeze tubes and standard caulk tube formats. Whichever type you choose, apply a generous bead to the crack, as shown in the top right photo.

Level surface with trowel. All that's left is to level the concrete patch with a mason's trowel, as shown in the bottom right photo. Use the trowel to feather the patch away from the edge to create a smooth surface. Note: If you don't have a mason's trowel, a stiff blade putty knife will work just fine.

Painting Floors

TOOLS

- Broom/vacuum
- Wire brush
- Paint tray and roller
- Paintbrush

When it comes to giving a floor a quick makeover, nothing beats paint. For just the cost of a gallon or two of paint, you can give a porch or patio floor an entirely new look. Just make sure to match the paint to the floor you're painting. Concrete (as shown here) requires special concrete paint—if you use regular paint, you won't get a good bond and the paint will quickly chip and peel off. Also, if traction is a concern, there are a number of anti-slip additives available for most paint.

Clean the floor. As with any painting job, the secret to success is proper preparation. Since a floor gets much more abuse than a wall or ceiling, this is especially important. For the paint to bond well with the existing floor, the surface must be clean and free from all debris. Start by sweeping or vacuuming the floor clean (bottom left photo). If you're planning on painting concrete, it's a good idea to clean the floor with household detergent or a chemical cleaner (see page 138 for more on this). If you choose to do this, make sure to rinse thoroughly and allow the concrete to dry completely before proceeding.

Deal with any cracks. If you're painting concrete, pay particular attention to any cracks. Hairline cracks (like the one shown in the bottom right photo) should be cleaned with a wire brush. Larger cracks should be repaired—see page 139 for step-by-step directions. Allow the concrete patch to fully dry before moving on to painting.

Mask as needed. The final bit of preparation work before breaking out the paint is to mask as needed. This includes adjacent walls, columns or railings, etc., that you don't want to paint. Painter's masking tape works well for this: It has less tendency to harm the underlying surface than standard masking tape (top right photo).

Paint around edges. When everything is masked, you're ready to paint. Start by working around the perimeter of the floor. You can use a trim pad with built-in rollers, or simply brush on the paint with a foam brush, as shown in the middle photo. Paint out from the wall about 2" to leave plenty of clearance for the paint roller. It's also best to paint around any obstacles such as columns and railings.

Roll on paint. Now you can paint the bulk of the floor with a roller. You'll want to use a long-nap roller for painting concrete, since the surface is rough. Start in one corner and roll out about a foot or two, working along one edge of the floor as shown in the bottom photo. Continue working in 1- to 2-foot strips until you reach the opposite wall. Take care to fully overlap your strokes to get even coverage. When you're done, allow the paint to dry completely and then go back and apply a second coat, again letting it dry completely before use.

Tiling a Floor

TOOLS

- Tape measure
- Notched trowel
- Tile saw
- Tile nipper (optional)
- Electric drill and mixing attachment
- Rubber mallet
- Grout float
- Bucket and sponge

Tiling is a do-it-yourself-friendly project that produces a good-looking and durable floor. Although similar in technique, tiling an exterior differs from interior work in the materials used. You'll need materials that can handle exposure to weather. This means using an exterior-grade thin-set mortar for attaching the tile, and selecting tile that will weather well. For most climates, your best bet is porcelain tile; stay away from ceramic tile, as it tends to crack easily in exterior applications. Keep in mind, though, that porcelain tile is trickier to cut than ceramic tile, because porcelain is much harder. A motorized tile saw is the way to go here—you can pick up homeowner versions for around $100, or you can rent a professional model at most home and tool rental centers.

Test the pattern. Select your tile, and order about 20% more than you'll need, to offset breakage and mis-cuts. Once you have the tile, the first thing to do is to test the tile pattern. Starting at one end of the slab (or in our case, the interior wall of the

sunroom), place tiles down until you reach the opposite end (top right photo). In most cases, you won't be able to cover the floor with full tiles and you'll have to cut partial tiles to fill in. Testing the pattern will show you roughly how wide you'll have to cut partial tiles. If you want the partial tiles to be the same width at each end, you'll need to find the centerpoint of the floor and re-lay the tiles, working out from the center.

Apply thin-set mortar. Where you start applying mortar to lay tile will depend on whether you're starting in a corner (as we did) or are working out from the center. Begin by mixing enough thin-set mortar to cover roughly a 4-foot-square area. Apply the mortar with the recommended-size notched trowel. Most mortar manufacturers suggest a $1/4" \times 3/8"$ notched trowel for 12" square tile. Start near the edges and pull the trowel toward you, keeping the trowel almost vertical to create uniform ridges (bottom right photo). Take care not to overwork the mortar, as this tends to dry it out. Continue applying mortar until you've filled about a 2-foot-square area.

Position full tiles. With the mortar applied, you can begin laying full tiles. Start in one corner (or at the centerpoint if you're working out from the center of the floor) and place the tile in the mortar (top photo). Press the tile gently into the mortar and wiggle it slightly back and forth as you continue to press gently down. What you're trying to accomplish here is an even distribution of mortar on the back of the tile. It's a good idea to lift a tile occasionally after you've placed it to check the back for a uniform coat of mortar. What you don't want to do is press the tile down so hard that the mortar squeezes out around the edges of the tile.

Use spacers as needed. Most tiles that are larger than 4" square require the use of cross-shaped spacers to create a uniform gap between the tiles for the grout. Flexible rubber spacers come in sizes ranging from 1/16" up to 1/2". Special T-shaped spacers are also available for tiling against a wall. Although designed to lay down flat, we find the spacers are easier to work with vertically, as shown in the middle photo. While this does require more spacers, they're much easier to remove once the tile is in place. As the tiles are set, you can reach back and pull the spacers out and reuse them.

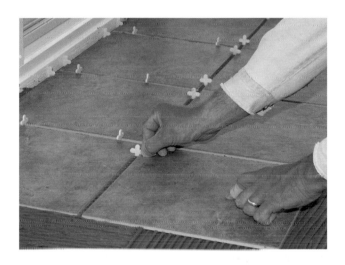

Set the tiles. As you complete a small section, stop and set and level the tiles. This is easily accomplished with a length of 2×4 wrapped with a scrap of carpeting. Lay the 2×4 diagonally across a couple of tiles at a time and tap it gently with a mallet, as shown in the bottom photo. Continue working across the tiles, tapping as you go. This will help set the tiles all at the same level and prevent any tiles from protruding. When you're done, start on a new section by applying mortar and tiles, then leveling them. Repeat until all the full tiles have been set.

Cut tiles as needed. When you reach the end of the floor and you need to cut partial tiles, measure the distance between the set tile and the end of the slab (or the wall) and subtract the width of two grout lines. Cut the tiles with a motorized tile saw, as shown in the top photo. As these require water to cool the diamond blade, it's best to cut these outside, where the mess is more easily contained. If you need to cut around an obstacle (such as a pipe), use a tile nipper. This pliers-like tool has sharp edges that let you nip off small pieces until the desired profile is reached. Take care to take small nips—larger nips usually result in too much tile being snapped off.

Install partial tiles. As you cut your partial tiles, you can install them, as shown in the middle photo. Because the motorized tile saw will soak the tiles with water, wipe off any excess before placing the tile; otherwise, the water can dilute the mortar and weaken the bond. When you've got a number of partial tiles placed, use the carpet-wrapped 2×4 to set and level them. Repeat for the remaining partial tiles. Allow the thin-set mortar to set up overnight to permanently lock the tiles in place.

Apply grout. Before you apply grout, go over the floor and check for spacers; remove any you find. Also, inspect the spaces between the tiles to make sure excess mortar has not filled the spaces. If you find spots where the mortar has squeezed out, remove the excess with a flat-blade screwdriver. Now you can mix up the grout—make only enough to cover a 5- to 6-foot-square area. You're looking for a consistency similar to oatmeal. Apply the grout with a grout float, and use the float to press the grout into the gap between the tiles, as shown in the bottom photo.

Squeegee off excess.

After you've grouted about a 3-foot-square area, go back and squeegee off the excess grout. Use the grout float held at about a 45-degree angle to the floor, as shown in the top photo. Work diagonally across the tile to keep the float from pulling out grout from between the tiles. Use firm pressure on the float for your final pass to remove as much grout from the tiles as possible—any grout remaining must be removed with a sponge as described below.

Clean with sponge.

Although not difficult, cleaning off the remaining grout is probably the most tedious part of tiling, as it takes time and patience. Start with a large bucket of clean water and a sponge. Wet the sponge and wring it out so it's just damp. Then gently wipe the sponge across the tiles, again working on diagonals, as shown in the middle photo, to keep from pulling out the grout from between the tiles. Rinse the sponge frequently— every tile or so—and change the water when it becomes cloudy. Continue sponging until all the excess grout has been removed and then move on to the next section. Repeat for the entire floor and allow the floor to dry.

Wipe off haze. After the floor dries, you'll probably see a thin film of grout on the tiles. Wipe off this haze with a clean, dry cloth, changing the cloth as necessary. Work in small 2-foot-square sections and continue until the tiles are clean and clear.

To keep the grout looking good over time, you'll need to seal it with a grout sealer; this is usually wiped on with a brush or special foam applicator. Make sure to wait the recommended time before applying this—typically two weeks—to make sure that all moisture evaporates. If you don't, you run the risk of sealing in moisture, which will eventually lead to mold.

Indoor/Outdoor Carpeting

Unlike standard carpeting, which must be stretched and fitted over tackless strips—a job that's best left to a pro—indoor/outdoor carpeting is a snap to install. There's no stretching involved, and the carpet is simply held in place with either adhesive or double-sided tape. Because indoor-outdoor carpet is exposed to the elements, and therefore takes a beating, it's best to attach it with double-sided tape. Although this doesn't bond the carpet to the underlying floor as securely as adhesive, it's a whole lot easier to replace the carpet when it eventually begins to fade and show wear. Although there are a number of products that look like indoor/outdoor carpet, make sure that you choose a type that is rated for outdoor use.

Position the carpet. To install indoor/outdoor

carpet on a concrete slab, start by vacuuming the concrete clean. Then unroll the carpet as shown in the bottom left photo, and roughly position it. What you're looking for here is a uniform overlap on all edges. Don't be tempted to position one of the cut carpet edges against a wall: Most edges aren't straight, and odds are, neither is the wall. For the optimum fit, you need some overlap so that you can cut the carpet to fit the wall, as described below.

Trim to fit. With the carpet roughly in place, start work on one edge. Press the carpet firmly into the corner with a metal straightedge, as shown in the bottom right photo. Then, while keeping firm pressure on the straightedge, run the blade of a utility or carpet knife along the straightedge to cut the carpet to fit the wall. Continue moving along the wall, cutting to fit.

Apply the double-sided tape. When you've got one wall cut, attach the carpet to the concrete with double-sided tape as shown in the top left photo. Make sure to use the thicker, stranded tape versus the thinner varieties. The thicker tape is better able to bridge small gaps between the carpet and the concrete and will do a better job over time holding it in place. Peel the backing off the tape and carefully reposition the carpet; press the carpet into the tape as you work along the wall. Then, to lock the carpet in place and keep it from shifting, roll back the carpet and make a large "X" with double-sided tape running from corner to corner.

Affix carpet to tape with roller. After you've peeled off the backing on the double-sided tape, roll the carpet back out and press the carpeting into the tape with a flooring roller, as shown in the bottom photo. A 75-pound roller can be rented from most home and tool rental centers for just a few dollars a day. Don't skip this important step—the roller is the best tool for getting a good carpet/tape bond.

Once you have the carpet fixed in place, go back and trim the remaining edges to fit, using the straightedge and knife. Secure the edges with double-sided tape.

Seam if necessary. For large areas, you may need to seam two smaller pieces together to fully cover the floor. In situations like this, it's best to fit one half of the carpet so it's attached to three sides, but not at the center. Then install the other half so it overlaps in the center. Here again, secure three sides. Now you can use a straightedge and utility knife to cut through both layers of carpet at once (as shown in the top right photo) to create a perfect seam. Roll each edge back and apply double-sided tape. Secure the carpet to the tape with the flooring roller.

8

EXTERIOR DOORS

In any deck, porch, or patio makeover, it's easy to overlook a key element: the exterior door opening into the house. We often get so used to an existing door that we don't even see it. But a new or made-over exterior door can have a huge impact on the overall makeover result. Sometimes, a fresh coat of paint or even just a new lockset will do the trick. For a totally new look, you can get real impact by replacing the door.

Fortunately, exterior doors come in a wide variety of styles, looks, and materials. That's because many homeowners want to make a personal statement with their front or entrance door—they want a door that's unique, like they are. Replacing an exterior door with a similarly sized door is easily accomplished by the average homeowner. All it takes is a bit of patience, some elbow grease, and a little know-how.

Painting an Exterior Door

TOOLS

- Wire brush
- Putty knife
- Paintbrush
- Roller and tray
- Screwdriver (optional)

You don't have to replace a door to get a new look—often all it takes is a fresh coat of paint. Exterior doors are usually constructed out of either solid wood, or metal that's filled with insulation. Solid-wood doors offer natural beauty and can easily be stained or painted to suit your tastes. Metal insulated doors offer better insulation properties than a solid-wood door, won't expand and contract with seasonal changes in humidity, and are considerably tougher than wood doors. These can also be painted to blend in with the home or to serve as an accent.

be exposed to the elements. Dirt on a door provides a way for moisture to work its way in; coupled with freeze/thaw cycles, this moisture can quickly cause the bond to fail and the paint to peel. Start by removing any loose dirt with a brass brush as shown in the bottom left photo; pay particular attention to the intricate details, as these are natural harbors for dirt. Then wash the door with a mixture of water and TSP (tri-sodium phosphate). TSP is available wherever paint is sold. Allow the door to dry completely before proceeding.

Clean the door thoroughly. Preparation is key when painting. This is particularly true for exterior surfaces that will

Mask or remove the lockset.
Before you paint the door, you'll need to either remove or mask off the handset. For round knobs like the one shown in the bottom right photo, masking works fine since it's easy to wrap a piece of tape around the base of the handset. For lever-type handsets, you'll be better off removing it, as the lever tends to get in the way of a roller.

Paint the details.

With the door masked, you can begin painting by starting with the details. Make sure to use a quality exterior paint for this job—oil-based paints tend to hold up better over time versus water-based paints. Also, if you're painting a dark door light, you'll be better off starting with a coat or two of white primer. Intricate details are best painted with a sash brush like the one shown in the top right photo. The angled tip of the brush makes it perfect for reaching into small lips and edges like the raised panel edges shown here. Paint all the details before covering the larger surfaces.

Mask the glass. If the door you're painting has any glass, you'll need to mask this off as well. Start by carefully masking off the glass, using 2"-wide masking tape to prevent accidents. An easy way to get tape to fit squarely in a corner is to use a putty knife as a straightedge to tear the tape, as shown in the top left photo. You'll also want to slip a drop cloth under the door to catch any drips or spills.

Paint the door.

Although you can paint the entire door with the sash brush, you'll find it'll go quicker with a small roller like the one shown in the bottom right photo. Rollers also tend to leave a smoother finish than brushes. Begin by painting the horizontal rails of the door. Then do the vertical stiles. As you complete a stile, make one final, full-length pass (also known as

striking off) to remove any brush, roller, or overlap marks. Let the paint completely dry before removing the tape and using the door.

Removing a Door

TOOLS

- Hammer and cold chisel
- Electric drill
- Screwdriver
- Prybar and cat's paw
- Putty knives
- Reciprocating saw or mini-hacksaw

If a fresh coat of paint won't help update the look of a door, it's time for a replacement. The first step in replacing an exterior door is to remove the existing door.

Remove the door from hinges. To remove a door, start by taking out the pins that hold the two halves of the door hinges together. You'll find it generally works best to start at the bottom hinge and work toward the top. Although most folks reach for a screwdriver and hammer to drive the pins out of the hinges, we recommend using a cold chisel instead. Some hinge pins can be extremely stubborn; the numerous hammer blows to a screwdriver will both mushroom the head and damage the tip. Reach for a cold chisel instead—it's designed for this kind of work. Once you've removed the pins, swing the door partially open so you can get a good grip on it. Lift up the door and set it aside as shown in the top photo.

Remove the hinge screws. When most doors are installed, one screw on each hinge jamb is removed (usually the center one) and replaced with a longer screw that will pass through the jamb and into the jack stud in the rough opening to firmly support the door. Instead of trying to cut through these screws in the next step, it's easier to simply remove them, as shown in the middle photo. If in doubt as to which hinge screws are the long ones, just remove them all.

TYPICAL WALL FRAMING WITH A ROUGH OPENING FOR A DOOR

■ A typical 2-by wall consists of vertical wall studs that run between the sole plate attached to the subfloor and the top plate or double top plate, as shown in the drawing. Whenever an opening is made in the wall for a window or door, a horizontal framing member called a header is installed to assume the load of the wall studs that were removed. The header is supported by jack studs (also referred to as trimmer studs) that are attached to full-length wall studs called king studs. The shorter studs that run between the header and the double top plate or from the underside of the rough sill of a window to the sole plate are called cripple studs.

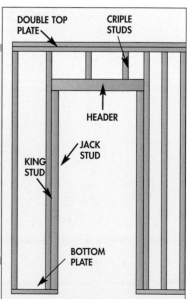

DOUBLE TOP PLATE
CRIPLE STUDS
HEADER
JACK STUD
KING STUD
BOTTOM PLATE

Remove interior trim. The next step in removing a door is to pry off the interior trim. How you do this will depend on whether or not you want to reuse the trim. If you're not planning on reusing it, a prybar and a putty knife will make quick work of the job, as shown in the top left photo. If, however, you want to salvage the trim, use two wide-blade putty knives. Slip both knives under the trim, then insert the prybar between the knives. The bottom putty knife will protect the wall covering while the other protects the trim as you lever it off with the prybar.

Remove exterior trim or nails. The trim that's attached to the outside of an exterior door is usually called brick molding. It's attached to the jamb and framing members with long finish nails known as casing nails. These casing nails can be removed either by prying off the brick molding or by pulling them out with a special type of prybar called a cat's paw. This tool is designed for removing nails flush or below the surface of a workpiece. A cat's paw has a small claw like a hammer, but it's curved at the end and comes to a point. This allows you to drive the claw into the trim so it captures the nail head. Then you simply lever out the nail as you would with a prybar or claw hammer, as shown in the middle photo.

Release jambs. With the trim removed or released from the framing, the next step is to release the doorjamb from the framing. Here again you can use a cat's paw to remove the nails, but if you have access to a reciprocating saw, you'll find it's a lot faster to simply cut the nails. Fit the saw with a demolition blade and slip it between the jamb and the framing, as shown in the top right photo. Since these saws are powerful and can buck hard when they come in contact with a nail, it's important to press the cutting guide of the saw firmly against the wall as you make the cut. Cut through the nails on both jambs.

Remove any threshold screws. The thresholds of most exterior doors are screwed to the flooring. A rubber seal running down the center of the threshold typically covers the screws. Pry this out with a screwdriver and then remove any screws holding the threshold in place, as shown in the top left photo.

Sever bond between frame and exterior.
There's one more thing to do before pulling out the jambs if you didn't remove the brick molding earlier—and that's to sever the caulk bond between the brick molding and the exterior wall cover-

ing. Caulk hardens over time, and if you don't cut through this, you run the risk of damaging the wall exterior when the jambs are removed. The caulk can be so tenacious that it can rip part of the wall covering away as the jambs are removed. Sever the old caulk bond with a utility knife or a putty knife, as shown in the bottom left photo.

Remove the jamb. At this point the jamb should be free of the framing members. All that's left is to pull it out of the opening. Since you'll probably encounter nails that have been cut off, it's a good idea to protect your hands with leather gloves. Grip one of the side jambs firmly and give it a tug to pull it out, as shown in the top right photo. After the jamb is removed, you can easily break it down for reuse or disposal.

A New Storm Door

It's a shame that many homeowners think of a storm door as they would a storm for a window—it's there just as a barrier to the elements. Sure, that's an important job. But the proper storm door can also serve as a decorative accent either to highlight the exterior door it covers (as shown here) or to hide a door that's a bit too ordinary. Storm doors are available in a wide variety of styles and colors. One of the more popular versions is the full-view storm like the one shown here.

Storm door anatomy. Most storm doors feature metal frames that house glass panes or screens or a combination of both, as shown in the drawing below. One feature to look for in a storm door is self-storing screens. That is, the screen/storm system works much like a storm window where the screen and storm panels are stored within the frame. Most storm doors are designed for either right-hand or left-hand installation—you control which way the door opens as you install the metal frame components of the door.

Remove the glass inserts. Depending on the type of storm door you've purchased, you may want to remove the glass panes or "inserts" from the frame. Most manufacturers suggest removing the glass insert only if it's self-storing. The advantage to this is it will lessen the weight of the door, making it a lot easier to move it around. Also, some doors are shipped with the frame temporarily attached to the door via a set of shipping clips.

STORM DOOR ANATOMY

BRICK MOLDING

DRIPCAP

Z-BARS

VENTILATING WINDOW

STATIONARY WINDOW

DOOR PANEL

INSECT SCREEN

SWEEP

place. Then go back and drill the remaining hinge holes and drive in the remaining screws, as shown in the top right photo.

Attach storm door to the jamb.

Now you're ready to attach the storm door to the jamb. Start by lifting up the door and positioning it in the frame opening according to the manufacturer's directions. When the hinge-side frame is snug against the jamb side of the molding, drive panhead screws through the pre-drilled holes in the face of the bar and into the brick molding on the exterior of the door, as shown in the bottom right photo.

Cut the frame pieces to fit. With the door prepared, the next step is to choose which way the door will open—either hinged right or hinged left. Once you've decided, you can size the frame pieces to fit your door opening. Follow the manufacturer's directions to measure the opening, and transfer this measurement to the hinge-side frame piece. Now you can cut the frame piece to length. Support the piece firmly on a sawhorse or other sturdy work surface and use a hacksaw fitted with a fine-tooth blade to cut each bar to length, as shown in the top left photo. When you're done, remove any sharp edges on the cut ends with a smooth mill file.

Attach the jamb trim to door. Now position the hinged frame piece on the edge of the door that you've selected to be the hinge side. Follow the manufacturer's instructions on how to position the bar on the door. Then use the specified drill bit to drill through the center hole of each hinge and into the door. Install one of the screws provided in the hardware kit into each of the hinges to lock them in

door with tape at the recommended position. Drill the holes (usually three) and remove the template. Then insert one half of the door latch into the holes you just drilled. Align the spindle that connects the operating mechanisms of both halves and slide the two halves of the latch together. Now insert the mounting screws and tighten them to draw the halves together, as shown in the bottom left photo. Next, align the spring-loaded strike on the side jamb opposite the latch and fasten it to the jamb with the screws provided. Since the plate is slotted, you can move it up or down as needed for it to engage the latch properly.

Secure the jamb trim. Next, open the door and drive the panhead screws supplied by the manufacturer into the pre-drilled holes in the side of the bar. These screws are installed in the jamb as shown in the top left photo. Be careful not to overtighten any of these screws, as they have a tendency to strip easily. Repeat these steps to install the latch-side frame piece and the header bar on top of the door frame.

Attach the strike plate. If your storm door uses a strike plate in lieu of a spring-loaded strike, attach the strike plate to the jamb as shown in the middle photo. Check for proper operation and adjust as needed.

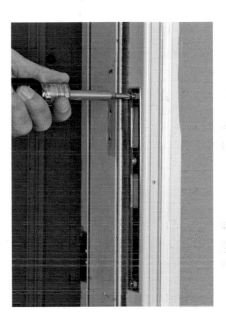

Install sweep. Finally, most storm doors come with a bottom expander or sweep to compensate for any variations at the threshold. Open the door and slip the expander over the bottom of the door. Then carefully insert the rubber sweep into the channel in the bottom of the door. Tip: To help the sweep slide in easily, apply a few drops of liquid detergent before inserting it.

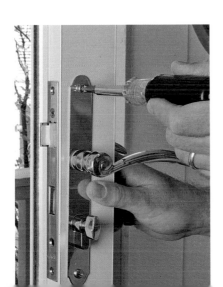

Install handset. Since storm doors are designed for both right- and left-hand use, the holes for the handset are not predrilled. Locate the drilling template in your door's instruction book and affix it to the

A New Exterior Door

A new exterior door can really liven up a deck, porch, or patio, particularly if you install one with decorative glass like the one shown here. To replace a door, first remove the old door (see pages 152–154). When it's time to shop for a replacement door, go with a pre-hung door. There are no mortises to cut, hinges to install, or holes to drill. All you need to do is slip the door into the rough opening, shim it so it's plumb and level, and nail it to the framing members. If it's so easy, why would you ever want to install a standard door? Standard doors are useful for odd-sized doors that need to be trimmed to fit, and when you just can't find the style of door you're looking for in a pre-hung. Most pre-hung doors come with the exterior brick molding already attached. If yours doesn't, it's best to attach molding to the jamb prior to installing the door. Brick molding is available pre-cut and pre-primed. All you need do is mark a reveal (typically 1/8") and nail the molding to the jamb.

Exterior door cross-section. A pre-hung exterior door fits into the rough opening in the outer wall. The threshold at the bottom of the door frame typically rests directly on the subfloor or is notched to fit over the subfloor and rests on the exterior framing (see the drawing at left). Most thresholds use a flexible rubber gasket to create a weathertight seal between the threshold and the bottom of the door. At the top of the door, brick molding is attached to the jamb and is covered with a drip edge to direct moisture away from the door. The space between the door frame (jambs) and the framing members of the rough opening is used to level and plumb the door via shims. In most cases, this space is later filled with insulation to reduce drafts.

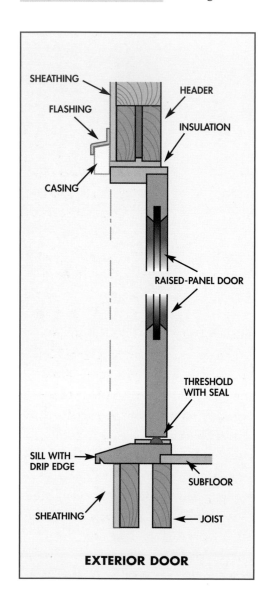

SHEATHING
FLASHING
CASING
HEADER
INSULATION
RAISED-PANEL DOOR
THRESHOLD WITH SEAL
SILL WITH DRIP EDGE
SUBFLOOR
SHEATHING
JOIST

EXTERIOR DOOR

Test the fit.

To make sure your new door will fit well in the rough opening, lift the door up and set it into the rough opening, as shown in the top left photo. Exterior doors tend to be heavy, so have a helper on hand to assist you as you lift and position the door. Once the door is in place, check to make sure you have sufficient clearance between both side jambs and the jack studs for the shims you'll use later to plumb and level the door. Be careful as you lift the door in and out of the opening not to catch the jamb on the framing members; it can easily splinter.

Insert the new door.

Now you can install the door. But before you do this, consider adding a little bit more insurance against the elements—apply a bead of silicone caulk on the back side of the brick molding. This caulk will help fill any gaps between the brick molding and the exterior wall covering. Note: You'll also caulk around the brick molding later once the door is completely installed. With the aid of a helper, lift the door up into position and use a 4-foot level to check it for plumb, as shown in the top right photo.

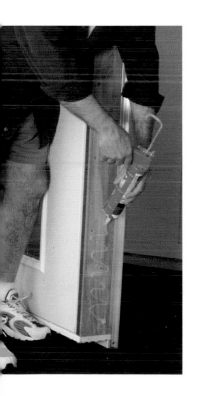

Seal the floor at the threshold.

Once you're sure the door will fit the rough opening, remove it and set it on its side. To create a seal under the threshold, either apply a generous bead of silicone caulk to the bottom of the threshold as shown in the bottom left photo, or apply a generous zigzag pattern directly onto the subfloor. Remember: It's a lot easier to wipe off excess caulk now than it is to remove the door after it's installed and then apply more caulk when you discover that the threshold leaks.

Shim as needed.

With the door plumb, the next step is to add shims to hold the door in place. This job is best done with a helper. One person holds and adjusts the position of the door in the rough opening and checks it for level and plumb, while the other inserts pairs of shims between the doorjambs and rough opening framing members, as shown in the middle photo. Start by inserting shims behind each of the three hinges, behind the opening for the plunger for the door lockset, and at the top and bottom of the latch-side jamb. Also insert pairs of shims at the center and both ends of the head jamb. Insert the shims in pairs of opposing wedges and adjust them in and out until they solidly fill the gap between the jamb and the framing members. Take your time here and double-check everything one more time before proceeding to the next step.

Nail through shims. Once you're satisfied that the door is level and plumb, you can secure it to the doorjamb. Your best bet here is 2 1/2"- to 3"-long hot-dipped galvanized casing nails. Make sure to drive the nails through the jamb only at the places where the shims are, as shown in the top right photo. The idea here is to drive the nail though the jamb and the shims into the framing members. This way the jamb will be fully supported. As you nail the jambs in place, check for plumb again with a level and adjust the shims if necessary.

Nail through brick molding on exterior.
Now you can secure the brick molding to the framing members. For this job, make sure that you use hot-dipped galvanized casing nails, typically 2 1/2" to 3" in length. Drive the nails through the face of the brick molding and into the framing member about every 12" or so, as shown in the middle photo. Then go back and countersink each nail with a nail set and fill the holes with exterior-grade putty.

Screw through hinges into jack stud. The pre-hung door you purchased should have come with three long hinge screws that are designed to lock the doorjamb firmly into the framing members. The door hinges may or may not have an empty slot waiting for these. If not, you'll need to remove one screw from each jamb hinge and replace it with a longer screw. If your door didn't come with these, purchase some 3"-long galvanized or coated deck screws and drive one into each hinge, as shown in the bottom right photo.

Cut off excess shims. To finish off the inside of the door, start by cutting off any protruding shims with a sharp utility knife, as shown in the top left photo. Then you can trim out the door with case molding; see pages 106–107 for more on installing trim. Before you install the trim, it's a good idea to insulate between the jamb and framing members as described below.

Insulate between jambs and framing. To keep out drafts and provide a barrier against heating and cooling losses, fill any gaps between the jambs and the framing members with insulation. Although you can force fiberglass insulation into the gaps with a putty knife, you'll find that foam will create a better seal (middle photo). The important thing is to purchase either window-and-door foam or minimal-expanding foam designed just for this. This special foam expands just a little compared to standard expanding foam. If you were to use standard expanding foam, the foam could expand to the point where it would cause the door to bind. Follow the manufacturer's directions about how much foam to shoot into the gaps.

Caulk around exterior trim. There's one more job to do on the exterior of the door, and that's to apply a bead of caulk around the perimeter of the brick molding. Using a high-quality paintable silicone caulk, apply a generous bead where the brick molding meets the siding, as shown in the bottom left photo. Fill in any gaps as needed with the caulk and then go back with a wet fingertip to smooth the caulk. Finally, install the lockset of your choice (see pages 162–163) and test the operation of the door. If all went well, it should open and close smoothly without binding and create a solid seal against the elements.

9

FINISHING TOUCHES

A bare deck, patio, or porch is like a Christmas tree without decorations—it's not until you add the details that it becomes something special. How will you personalize your outside space: with some simple scrollwork ornamentation? By adding an elegant, custom handrail? It all depends on the look and functionality you want, of course, and whether you follow the credo "less is more"—or "more is more."

In this chapter we'll show you several options: how to make a simple site-built planter that attaches to an existing railing to showcase your favorite flowers; how to install wood, vinyl, or composite handrails; how to add a trellis with climbing plants; and how to install simple exterior lighting like a new porch light or low-voltage lighting. This way, you can pick and choose the makeover details that will fit—and reflect—your personal style.

A Railing Planter

TOOLS

- Hand or circular saw
- Drill and bits
- Tape measure
- Putty knife
- Hammer/nail set
- Screwdriver

A classic way to add a splash of color to a deck, porch, or patio is with flowers. Although you can place plants in a container on the floor, they'll be a lot more visible in a planter that rests on a rail, as shown in the top photo. Yes, you can purchase a pre-made planter, but they can be expensive and often aren't sized for your railing. The planter shown here can be custom-made to fit your rail. Because of its simple design, it's easy to alter the dimensions of the planter to suit your needs.

The railing planter consists of a front and back, two sides, and a bottom—all cut from 1×6 pine; see the exploded drawing below. (Note: Cedar and redwood are both excellent choices for this project, as they are naturally weather- and rot-resistant.) The sides are 5$\frac{1}{2}$" wide, and the front and back can be cut to any length. The bottom is also a length of 1×6 cut to fit inside the box once it's assembled.

Assemble the sides and front. To make the railing planter, begin by cutting the ends and sides to length. Then apply a generous coat of glue to the sides and attach the front and back to them with 1$\frac{1}{2}$" hot-dipped galvanized nails, as shown in the bottom photo. Set the nails below the surface of the wood with a nail set and fill the holes with putty.

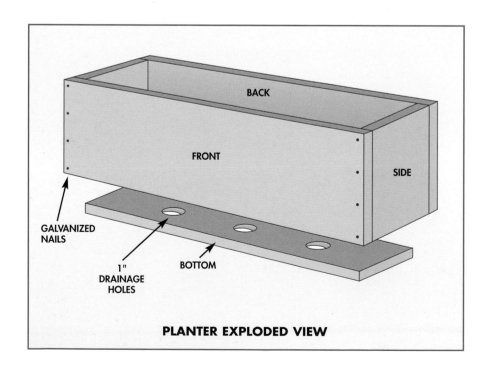

GALVANIZED NAILS

1" DRAINAGE HOLES

BACK

FRONT

SIDE

BOTTOM

PLANTER EXPLODED VIEW

Add the bottom. With the box assembled, the next step is to add the bottom. Just measure the inside length of the assembled box and cut a bottom to fit. Attach it to the front, back, and sides with glue and nails as shown in the top photo. Allow the glue to set overnight before proceeding.

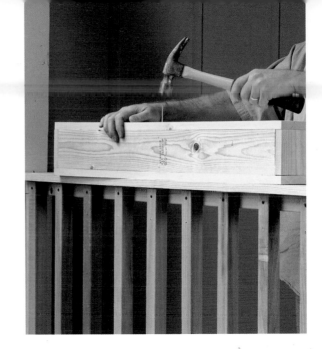

Attach the planter to the railing. Once the glue has dried, place the planter on the railing in the desired location so the planter is centered on the width of the railing. Then secure it to the railing by driving 2" galvanized deck screws through the bottom of the planter and into the railing, as shown in the middle photo.

Drill a set of drainage holes. To prevent the planter from filling with water from rain or overwatering, you'll want to drill a series of drainage holes in the bottom of the planter. If the railing you've attached it to is wood (like the one shown here), you can simply drill through the bottom of the planter and through the railing. Use a 1" spade bit and drill to center holes every 12" or so, as shown in the bottom photo. If you can't drill through the railing, drill a series of smaller holes around the inside perimeter of the planter to allow it to drain.

Coat the inside with roofing cement.

Since the wood inside the planter will be constantly exposed to moisture and dirt, it's best to seal it completely so it won't mold, decay, and rot over time. An easy way to waterproof the inside of the planter is to coat the inside with roofing cement. This viscous and rather smelly stuff is best applied with a disposable plastic putty knife, as shown in the top photo. Make sure to wear rubber gloves when you apply this and allow it to fully harden before adding soil and plants.

Prepare for the plants.

Once the roofing cement has hardened, you can prepare the planter for your plants. The first step is to add rocks in the bottom of the planter to encourage drainage, as shown in the inset photo below. A 1" layer will work fine. Then you can add 3" to 4" of potting soil, as shown in the bottom left photo.

Add the plants. All that's left is to add the plants. Place them roughly where you want them and then remove the plants from their plastic containers, as shown in the top right photo. Set the plants in the potting soil and carefully fill around them with more potting soil. Give the plants a thorough watering and enjoy.

Planting Shrubs

Shrubs can help increase the value of your property and provide privacy and beauty around your home. They can add a splash of color or even hide a less-desirable feature of a deck, porch, or patio, such as the understructure of a deck. The type of shrub you choose will depend on your climate, the look you're after, your soil, and the exposure the plant will enjoy. For help choosing a shrub, contact a gardening professional at your local home and garden center. Shrubs come in three planting styles: bareroot, balled-and-burlapped, and, the most common, container.

The big advantage of using a plant grown in a container is that 100% of the roots are in the container. This way the plant undergoes only limited transplant shock if given adequate follow-up care. Plus, container-grown plants can be planted into the landscape year-round. The big disadvantage of container-grown plants is the possibility of deformed roots. Plants that are "rootbound" have roots circling around inside the container. These entangled roots will hamper future growth. What size shrub you choose will depend on the look you're after and your budget. It's important to know that smaller plants thrive better and establish faster than large plants—plus, they're a lot cheaper.

If possible, plant your shrubs as soon as you get them home. Otherwise, they may dry out and be injured. If you can't plant them immediately, place the shrubs in a shady or sheltered spot. Cover the roots of bareroot shrubs with moist soil, sand, or peat moss. Keep the soil of balled-and-burlapped or container plants moist until planting.

Locate rough position of the shrubs. The first step in planting shrubs is to roughly locate their position. With container plants this is easy to do by simply plac

ing the plants in their rough positions, as shown in the middle photo. Follow the grower's label directions on spacing and distance from structures (or ask your local garden pro). Also, make sure that shrubs you've chosen are appropriate for the sun exposure (full, partial, shady) of their new location.

Excavate. Next, dig a hole at least twice the diameter of the shrub's root-ball, as shown in the bottom photo. Don't dig too deep—once the plant is set in the hole, the top of the roots or root ball should be level or slightly above level with the ground. It's better to plant the shrub raised so the roots will not drown or suffocate. Be sure to remove tags, wires, or ropes from the stems. These can strangle and kill the plant as it grows.

Add drainage if needed. Since too much moisture can reduce plant growth and even kill the shrub, you should plant in well-drained soil. To test for soil drainage, dig the hole for your new plant and fill it with water. If necessary, add pebbles or sand to help water drain, as shown in the top photo. If the water doesn't drain in 24 hours, plant elsewhere. If, on the other hand, the soil is sandy and moisture leaches out quickly, a heavier topsoil can be added. Adding organic matter can help improve the water-holding capacity of the sandy soil.

Add some fertilizer. Applying the correct fertilizer at planting helps keep the shrub healthy. Use a slow-release fertilizer, preferably composed of 25 to 50% water-insoluble nitrogen (WIN), into the soil backfill at planting time, as shown in the bottom left photo. If the shrubs are to be mass-planted in a bed or where the entire planting area can be worked, incorporate 3 to 5 inches of organic matter into the entire bed to the depth equal to the height of the root-ball.

Position the shrub. With a container-grown shrub, it can be tricky to remove the container from the root-ball. It's a good idea to give the plants a thorough watering the night before you plant. If it's too dry, the root-ball could fall apart on you when planting. With small 1- to 2-gallon containers, you just get a grip on the top of the root-ball and then turn it upside down. Once it's flipped over, just tap the sides to loosen the container, grab the container and let the root-ball slide out. For larger containers, lay them on their side, rap on the sides, and pull the container off. You can also cut the container off. Also, container-grown roots tend to grow in circles. So before planting, take a knife and make four or five vertical cuts down the roots to get them growing out again. Then place the shrub so it's centered in the hole, as shown in the middle photo.

Backfill around the shrub. With the shrub in place, you can replace the soil in the hole, as shown in the top photo. If your original soil, or backfill, contains too much rock or construction debris, replace it with local topsoil. Backfill should, in most cases, be the soil removed from the planting hole: "What comes out...goes back in." Avoid replacing topsoil with straight organic matter. When the hole is about three-fourths refilled, level and turn the plant if necessary; tamp the soil down gently. Water the shrub heavily to eliminate air pockets. Then finish filling the hole with backfill to its original level. Use excess soil to build a berm or ring about 6" from the outside edge of the hole. Then water heavily again.

Add some mulch. After you've planted the shrub, add a 3" to 4" layer of organic mulch on the surface around the shrub. Mulch helps conserve moisture, discourage weeds, and moderate soil temperatures. And, it looks good. Place mulch (pine needles, straw, bark chips, or slightly decomposed or shredded leaves) 2" or 3" deep around the shrub, as shown in the middle and bottom left photos. Avoid overly deep mulch or piling the mulch up against the trunk of the shrub, which promotes shallow roots, disease, and injury from pests.

Distribute mulch. As you distribute the mulch, construct a dam 4" to 6" high around the shrub after planting, as shown in the middle right photo. This will help moisture to collect in this "saucer" and move slowly down into the planting hole, minimizing runoff. Water is absolutely essential for new plants. You want to soak them for the first week to help them get established. Then, back off so they don't get too much water, which can create problems after that first week.

A Wood Handrail

TOOLS

- Hand or circular saw
- Electric drill and bits
- Tape measure and level
- Screwdriver
- Paintbrush

Regardless of the type of decking you have—wood, composite, or vinyl—a wood handrail can complement the deck. You can stain the handrail to match the decking, or stain/paint it to contrast and serve as an accent. Although you can build a handrail using standard 2-by pressure-treated lumber, cedar, or redwood, we chose a handrail system that uses ready-made components; this makes assembly quick and easy.

The handrail system shown here attaches to any posts via a set of brackets—one to connect the handrail to the post at the top and one to connect it at the bottom. What makes this system unique is that the rails are grooved to accept wood strips that you attach to the balusters. After you install the bottom rail, the baluster/wood-strip assembly simply slips into the groove in the bottom rail. Then you add the top rail to create an almost instant handrail.

Drill holes in the posts. The most common method for attaching posts to a deck is to secure them to the rim joist with bolts as shown here (for alternative methods, see page 51). In most cases, posts that will be attached to the rim joists are notched at the bottom so the posts will extend over the deck. To mount these posts, you'll need to drill a set of holes for the bolts that hold them in place. The most accurate way to do this is to build a simple drilling jig as described on page 173. Place the jig on the post so the end is flush with the post. Then clamp or grip it to prevent it from shifting, and drill the holes through the notched end of the post, as shown in the bottom photo.

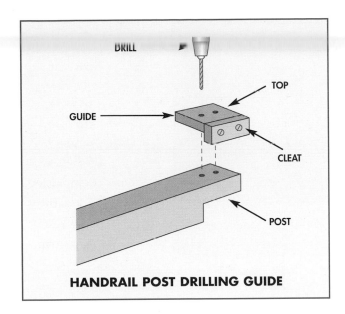

HANDRAIL POST DRILLING GUIDE

Post drilling guide. The post drilling guide is just a pair of wood scraps glued and screwed together (see the drawing above). Cut the top to match the width of the post, and lay out and drill a pair of centered holes in the top to fit the bolts you'll be using. Then glue and screw a cleat onto the side of the top to serve as a stop.

Attach the posts. To attach a post to the rim joist, first position the post where you want it and check it for plumb. Then drill through the holes you just drilled and into the rim joist. If you're using bolts, use the same size bit as you used to drill the holes in the post. If you're planning on using lag screws, make sure to use a smaller drill bit, as all you want to drill here is a pilot hole for the bolt. After you've drilled both holes, thread a pair of bolts (or lag screws) through the post and/or rim joist and tighten them, making sure that the post is plumb as you tighten, as shown in the bottom left photo. Repeat for all the other posts.

Attach the rail brackets. Once you have all the posts installed, you can work your way around the perimeter of the deck, attaching brackets to the lower end of the posts, as shown in the top right photo. To get consistent spacing, consider using a scrap of wood as a spacer to position each bracket before screwing it in place.

Add the bottom railing. Now you can add the railing, working on one section at a time. Measure the distance between the bottom brackets and cut a length to fit, as shown in the bottom right photo. With the groove in the rail facing up, secure the rail to the brackets by driving in screws up through the brackets and into the rail. Make sure to use weather-resistant screws, such as hot-dipped galvanized or stainless steel screws. Repeat this for the remaining bottom rail sections.

Baluster tip. An alternative to spacing out and installing the balusters that doesn't rely on marking each baluster is to use a spacer, as shown in the top right photo. The only thing you'll have to mark with this method is the center of each strip. Then install the center baluster. Use the spacer to position the remaining balusters by butting it up against a baluster and sliding in another baluster so it presses firmly against the spacer. If you have access to an air-powered stapler, you can build the baluster assemblies in minutes using the spacer.

Assemble the baluster sections. With all the bottom rails installed, you can build the baluster assemblies, working on one section at a time (top left photo). Begin by measuring between the posts and cutting a pair of strips to this length. Then mark the center of the strips and lay out baluster locations on both strips at the same time, every 4 1/2" on center. (Check your local building code to make sure you're meeting the maximum baluster spacing requirements.) Then secure the balusters to the strips with small weather-resistant screws, nails, or staples.

Attach the top railing. After you've finished a baluster assembly, set it into the groove in the bottom rail. Then measure and cut a top rail to fit between the posts. Place this on top of the baluster assembly and drive a couple of screws up through the top strip of the baluster assembly and into the handrail, as shown in the bottom right photo. Now you can secure the top rail to the posts by attaching brackets under the rail, as you did at the bottom. When all of the railing is up, apply the stain or paint of your choice.

METAL BALUSTERS

Here's an interesting twist on the classic wood handrail—replace the wood balusters with metal versions to give your deck a one-of-a-kind look.

The folks at Deckorators (www.deckorators.com) offer a number of maintenance-free aluminum deck balusters that let you create a deck rail that reflects your personal style. Their deck balusters come in three different series (see the photos below) that offer a variety of colors to provide many design options. Deckorators' balusters can easily be installed to either wood or composite products to create beautiful deck railings. Each architectural aluminum baluster stands $32^1/2$" and comes with four matching screws.

Deckorators also offers a number of products that simplify handrail construction. These include: baluster connectors, which install on the top and bottom of the deck rails to create a perfect connection between the top and bottom deck rail; stair connectors designed to work with deck rails for stairs between 30 and 35 degrees; and railing connectors that create a strong and effective support to the deck rail. These railing connectors eliminate the need to toenail the wood into the post, creating a clean and secure rail.

Classic: The classic-style balusters offer the look of simple wrought-iron bars and are available in seven different colors. The handrail can be spiced up by using distinctive centerpieces.

Colonial: Colonial balusters resemble turned posts that were common on fences and handrails of old. Used by themselves or combined with classic balusters, they create a unique, charming handrail.

Architectural: For the ultimate in distinctive handrails, consider using one of the two architectural baluster designs available. Both provide the look of wrought iron, yet each offers a different look.

A Vinyl Handrail

Want the look of a pristine painted-white handrail, but without the effort? Consider a vinyl handrail. Not only are these systems remarkably easy to install, but they also require virtually no maintenance or upkeep over time. Additionally, unlike a wood handrail, there's never any worry about getting splinters from the vinyl version. And because of their building-block-style construction, there's no measuring when it comes time to install the balusters—precut holes make installation a snap.

Locate and attach the post brackets.

The first step to installing a vinyl handrail is to locate and attach the post brackets. On a typical vinyl handrail system, these brackets attach directly to the deck and the post is inserted in them and screwed in place. On other systems, the vinyl posts are actually sleeves that slip over preexisting posts, much like those used in a composite rail system as described on pages 179–180. Locate a post bracket at each corner of the deck and in between these as specified by the manufacturer (in most cases, the handrails are made in 6- or 8-foot lengths, so this is the maximum length they can span). At each location,

screw the bracket to the deck with weather-resistant screws as shown in the bottom left photo.

Vinyl rail system. A typical vinyl handrail system consists of three main parts: the posts, the top/bottom rails, and the balusters. On most systems, the top and bottom rails are identical and have precut holes for the balusters. The top and bottom rails attach to the post via a set of vinyl brackets. The post sits in a post bracket or anchor, which is usually covered with a cap to hide the screws. The top of the post accepts a post cap. These range from simple (as shown here) to elaborate.

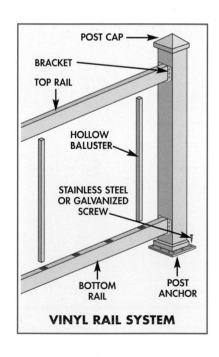

VINYL RAIL SYSTEM

- POST CAP
- BRACKET
- TOP RAIL
- HOLLOW BALUSTER
- STAINLESS STEEL OR GALVANIZED SCREW
- BOTTOM RAIL
- POST ANCHOR

Install the posts and the bracket covers. After you've installed the post brackets, you can work around the deck perimeter, installing the posts. Start by inserting a post in a bracket as shown in the top right photo. Then slip the bracket cover (if applicable) over the post and down onto the post bracket as shown in the inset photo. These covers typically snap in place on top of the post bracket.

Attach the bottom rails. Once all the posts are in place, you can begin installing the bottom rails. Working on one section at a time, measure the distance between the posts and cut a piece of handrail to length. Take care to make sure the baluster holes are evenly spaced at the ends. (Note: Some manufacturers may direct you to subtract $1/8"$ or so from your measurement before cutting the rail to length to allow for expansion.) Once you've cut a rail to length, attach it to the posts with the brackets supplied, as shown in the middle photo. For accurate spacing, cut a scrap block to insert under each rail end to position the rail up the desired distance from the bottom.

Add the balusters. With the bottom rail in place, now you can insert the balusters in the precut holes as shown in the bottom photo. As you do this, make sure that each baluster seats all the way in the hole so that it bottoms out inside the rail.

Add the top rails. Adding the top rails is definitely the trickiest part to assembling a vinyl handrail. That's because you need to align all the balusters with the precut holes on the rail. The most reliable method we found to do this was to start at one end and slowly work toward the other, fitting in each baluster in sequence, as shown in the top photo. This takes a little patience and can be greatly speeded up if you have a helper. The important thing is to keep firm, constant pressure on the end you started with, to prevent the rail from rocking and pulling out the balusters you've already inserted.

Attach the top rails. When all the balusters fit in the holes in the top rail, you can secure the top rail to the post with the brackets supplied. This is just a matter of driving weather-resistant screws through the bracket and into the post, as shown in the middle photo. Before you secure the opposite end of the rail, take the time to make sure the top rail is level.

Finish off with the end caps. All that's left is to install the post caps. These are simply pressed onto the top of the posts, as shown in the bottom photo. If desired, run a small bead of silicone caulk inside the rim of the post cap before pressing it onto the post. This will create a watertight and bug-proof seal as well as serving as an adhesive to keep the cap in place over time.

A Composite Handrail

TOOLS

- Circular or miter saw
- Tape measure
- Try or combination square
- Electric drill and bits
- Screwdriver
- Calculator

Although composite decking has been around for a while, it's only been in the last couple of years that some composite manufacturers have started offering matching handrails. The composite deck and handrail shown here are made by TimberTech (wwwtimbertech.com) and offer beauty, ruggedness, and best of all, virtually no maintenance or upkeep. The composite material—a mixture of plastics and wood dust—will age gracefully over time. The only maintenance required is spraying it off once a year with a hose to wash away any dirt and debris.

Cover the posts and attach the balusters.

The TimberTech railing system can use either preexisting posts or new ones—the posts are actually composite sleeves that slip over a wood post. If your deck doesn't currently have posts, see post-mounting options on page 51 and use the instructions and jig on pages 172–173 to attach them to your deck. Then slip a post sleeve over each post, as shown in the bottom left photo. Next, use weather-resistant screws to mount a baluster, screwing through the post sleeve and into the post, as shown in the inset photo at left. Note the use of the spacer block to accurately position the baluster up the recommended distance from the deck.

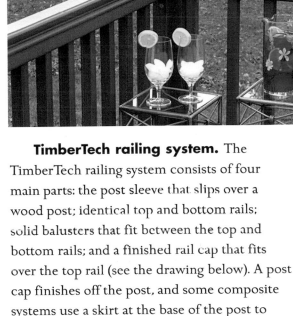

TimberTech railing system. The TimberTech railing system consists of four main parts: the post sleeve that slips over a wood post; identical top and bottom rails; solid balusters that fit between the top and bottom rails; and a finished rail cap that fits over the top rail (see the drawing below). A post cap finishes off the post, and some composite systems use a skirt at the base of the post to serve as a transition. Balusters are screwed to the posts and accept the rails and baluster assembly.

The top and bottom rails are screwed to the balusters attached to the posts to hold them in place. The rail cap is secured by driving screws up through the top rail and into the rail cap.

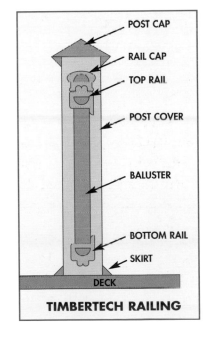

POST CAP

RAIL CAP

TOP RAIL

POST COVER

BALUSTER

BOTTOM RAIL

SKIRT

DECK

TIMBERTECH RAILING

Lay out the baluster locations. Laying out the balusters is the biggest challenge to installing a composite rail system. With the TimberTech system, work on one section at a time by first measuring the distance between two posts (A). Then subtract 1.35" to get the distance between the posts from the center of the post-mounted balusters (B). Divide this number by 5 and round up to the next highest number. This is the number of spaces you'll have between the posts (C). Now divide B by C to determine baluster spacing. This number should not exceed 5". After you've determined baluster spacing, cut two pieces of top/bottom rail to fit between the posts. Then mark a centerline on both rails and lay out the balusters, working from the center out toward the ends, as shown in the top photo.

Attach the balusters. To attach the balusters, first drill pilot holes for the screws at each baluster location in both rails. Then, working on one rail at a time, drive a screw up through the rail and into the baluster. Be sure to hold the baluster firmly in place as you drive in the screw, as shown in the middle photo. When you have all the balusters attached to one rail, attach the opposite rail to the balusters, making sure the rail fronts are facing in the same direction.

Mount the rails to the posts. Once a rail section has been assembled, you can attach it to the posts. Just slip the ends of the top/bottom rails over the balusters mounted to the posts (a helper makes this a lot easier). Then secure the rail assembly to the post balusters by driving a screw through the rail ends into the balusters, as shown in the bottom photo. Repeat for the remaining sections. Finish off the railing by adding the post caps. These are best secured to the posts by running a bead of silicone caulk around the inside perimeter of the cap before placing it on the post.

COMPOSITE STEPS

■ If your deck has steps and you're working with composite decking, you can cover the stairs with the same materials. Installation is very similar to the decking as described on pages 96–99.

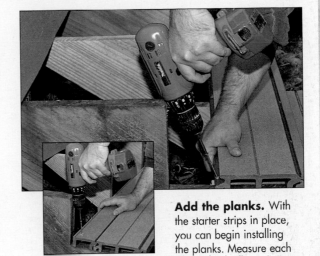

Add the planks. With the starter strips in place, you can begin installing the planks. Measure each step individually and cut planks to length. Install the first plank by inserting the tongue on the plank into the groove in the starter strip. Drive a screw through the back edge of each plank into the riser, as shown in the top right photo. Cut the next plank to width as needed to fit into the remaining space and secure it to the riser with screws, as shown in the inset photo. Repeat for all the steps.

Install the starter strip. Begin by measuring the distance between the risers, and cut a starter strip to length for each step. Then attach this strip to the front edge of the risers with the groove facing in toward the steps, as shown in the top left photo. Repeat for each step.

Add the trim. You can stop at this point or you can add some trim. Cut fascia planks to width and length to fill in the backs of the steps, as shown in the bottom photo. Secure these pieces to the risers with screws. Additionally, you can cover the sides of the risers—and the exposed ends of the planks—by cutting fascia to length and width and securing these to the sides of the end risers.

Adding a Trellis

TOOLS
- Hammer
- Drill and bits
- Screwdriver

A trellis is an inexpensive way to add both privacy and color (via some climbing plants) as part of a deck, porch, or patio makeover. You can purchase pre-made trellises at most home and garden centers—typically made from cedar or redwood—or you can make your own by simply nailing together strips of wood into any configuration you want. Although many trellises are left natural, you can stain or paint yours any color you'd like.

Secure the base. There are usually a couple of ways to secure the bottom of a trellis. The simplest is to push the bottom ends of the trellis into the soil. For a more secure method, consider attaching the trellis to a stake driven in the ground. Use a rot-resistant wood (such as cedar) and drive the stake in the soil at the center of the trellis, as shown in the top right photo. Then screw the trellis to the stake (inset photo above).

Secure the top. To protect your trellis—and your plants—from damage due to high winds, it's a good idea to secure the top of your trellis, if possible. In most cases, this can be done by driving a screw or nail through one of the top pieces of the trellis into the wall or the trim that the trellis rests against, as shown in the bottom right photo.

Position the trellis.

The first step to installing a trellis is to place it where you want it. Start by roughly positioning the trellis and then take a couple of steps back and see how it looks (bottom left photo). Try to envision the trellis covered with climbing plants. Adjust as necessary until you've located the perfect spot.

Position the plant. Start by locating the best position for your climbing plant. In most cases, this will be in the center of the trellis for a single plant, as shown in the top photo. If you're planting multiples, space them evenly along the base of the trellis. Mark the center of each plant location with a stick or rock.

Excavate and plant. After you've located where you want your plant or plants, you can excavate. Dig a hole that's 3 times the width of the container that the plant came in, as shown in the bottom left photo. Excavate deep enough so that when the plant is in place, the top of the root-ball will rest slightly above ground level. Then combine planting mix or potting soil and existing soil, and fill around the plant to ground level. Do not tamp the soil down. Then form a basin around the plant with a 2" mound of soil. Water the soil to settle, and add more soil if needed. Then cover the root-ball with 1" to 2" of mulch.

CLIMBING PLANTS

■ Although you can leave a trellis bare, most folks like the look of a leaf- or flower-covered trellis. There is a big variety of climbing plants available at most home and garden centers and nurseries. Look for plants that are clearly labeled as climbing plants. If in doubt, ask for help identifying which plants would be right for your trellis. The plant shown here is a Shiro Ban Akebia, which is a vigorously spreading and twining vine. It displays a bluish green foliage with dangling stalks of highly fragrant white flowers.

Help the plant to climb. With the plant firmly in the ground, remove any sticks used to support the vines and gently weave the vines in and out of the trellis, as shown in the right photo. This will help train the plant to grow where you want it to grow. Check periodically throughout the growing season, and thread any straying vines back onto the trellis as needed.

Low-Voltage Lighting

Whether you're looking for some added outdoor ambience or simply want to illuminate a pathway, low-voltage lighting is the answer. Low-voltage lighting is one of the more homeowner-friendly home improvement projects, especially if you buy a low-voltage lighting kit—which we highly recommend. Although you can purchase parts individually, a lighting kit has all you need in a single box. The only requirement is that there be a GFCI-protected outlet nearby. Other than that, it's really a matter of assembling the lights, running a cable, and plugging it in. Be careful as you shop for these kits: The lower-priced units are mostly plastic and tend not to stand up well over time. Invest in quality metal lights.

Assemble the lights. To install a low-voltage lighting system, start by following the manufacturer's directions to assemble the individual lamp fixtures. This can be as simple as attaching an already-assembled light onto its stake-like base, or as complex as having to insert a wiring harness into the lamp holder. Install the lamp, add the diffuser, and attach the base, as shown in the middle photo. Be especially careful when attaching the wiring harness, as the metal pin connectors are fragile and damage easily. If you have to use force to install one, don't; that's a sign of something wrong—either you're installing it incorrectly or the lamp holder or harness is defective.

Typical low-voltage lighting system. A typical low-voltage lighting system consists of three main parts: a low-voltage power transformer and timer unit that plugs into a weatherproof receptacle; a low-voltage power cable that transports low-voltage electricity to the lights; and a set of lights with snap-on connectors that attach to the low-voltage cable (see the bottom drawing). Each lamp fixture usually has

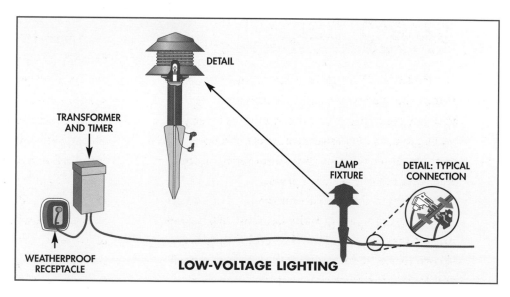

TRANSFORMER AND TIMER

DETAIL

LAMP FIXTURE

DETAIL: TYPICAL CONNECTION

WEATHERPROOF RECEPTACLE

LOW-VOLTAGE LIGHTING

a number of parts. These include the stake-like base section that's inserted in the soil, a lamp holder and diffuser, and a top or cap to keep out the weather. Depending on what you buy, you may or may not have to assemble the lamp fixtures.

Run the cable. After you've positioned all the lights, you can run the power cable. Start at the farthest light away from the outdoor receptacle and run the cable back toward the receptacle, as shown in the top right photo. Run the cable loosely—don't stretch it. You'll need a little slack when you go to hide the cable in the soil later.

Position the lights. One of the really nice things about a low-voltage lighting system is that you can pretty much put the lights wherever you want them, as long as you can route the power cable to them. You can space them out evenly or concentrate them in one or more areas.

Start by roughly positioning the lamps where you want them. Just grip the lamp by its base and press it into the soil at the desired location, as shown in the middle left photo. Take a step back and look at the placement; adjust as necessary.

Connect the lights to the cable. With the cable in place, you can connect the lights. Virtually all low-voltage lighting systems use a two-piece snap-together connector; each half fits on one side of the power cable, as shown in the middle right photo. When the two halves of the connector are squeezed together, sharp prongs inside the connector halves pierce the insulation of the power cable to make a solid electrical connection. Additionally, most connectors have some kind of positive indicator when the two halves are squeezed together sufficiently to guarantee a good connection. Do this for each of the lights.

Bury the cable. Now that all the connections have been made, you can work your way from light to light, hiding the cable. In most cases all this entails is digging a shallow trench in the soil, inserting the cable, and covering it up. If the area that you're working in is covered with mulch, this is an even simpler task. Just brush some of the mulch aside, insert the cable, and recover with the mulch, as shown in the top photo.

Connect the cable to power. All that's left is to connect the power cable to the low-voltage transformer and plug it in. On most kits, the power cable is already stripped. All you need do is follow the manufacturer's directions to secure the cable to the transformer terminals. These may be push-in or snap-in terminals, or screw terminals like those shown in the middle photo. Once connected, attach the transformer to the wall nearest the receptacle (these usually hang on one or two screws driven into the wall), and plug the transformer's power cord into the receptacle. Note: If the receptacle is exposed to the elements, you'll need to install a weatherproof cover—these are available wherever electrical supplies are sold.

Set the timer. Finally, follow the manufacturer's directions on setting the timer. This usually entails placing a set of plastic stops along the edge of a rotating timer at the desired on and off intervals, as shown in the bottom left photo.

Adding Lattice

Want instant privacy for your deck, porch, or patio? Add some lattice. These simple and inexpensive pre-made panels are available at most home and garden centers in a variety of materials, including pressure-treated lumber, cedar, redwood, and plastic (usually in white or green). Lattice is very easy to install and can provide just the right amount of privacy while still allowing plenty of ventilation.

Attach the stiles. To install lattice between the posts or columns of a deck, porch, or patio, start by attaching a pair of 2-by stiles to each post or column. These should match the width of the lattice (typically 48") and can be secured with galvanized or vinyl-coated deck screws. In most cases, you'll want to center the stiles on the posts or columns, as shown in the middle left photo.

Measure for the lattice. With the stiles installed, you can determine the size of the lattice. Start by measuring from post to post and then subtract 1/4" for clearance, as shown in the bottom left photo. Then measure the lattice and cut it to this length.

Position the lattice against the stiles and attach it to the stiles with weather-resistant screws, as shown in the bottom right photo. Three or four screws per side should do the job. Just be sure to drill pilot holes in the lattice before driving in the screws to prevent the lattice from splitting. After you've secured both sides, cut a 2-by cap to fit across the top of the lattice and secure it to the stiles with screws, as shown in the inset photo.

A New Porch Light

TOOLS

- Screwdriver
- Plastic putty knife (optional)
- Wire strippers (optional)

A simple way to dress up a deck, porch, or patio is to replace an existing outdoor light fixture with a new one. Since power has already been run to the existing fixture, it's really just a matter of removing the old and mounting the new. When you go to purchase a new light, make sure the one you purchase is designed for exterior use and that it will fit in the space allowed.

Remove the old fixture.
To install a new porch light, start by removing the old fixture. First turn off the power at the breaker or fuse panel and tag it so no one inadvertently turns it back on while you're working on the light. Then remove the bulb and old diffuser. Loosen the mounting screws or nuts and pull the old fixture away from the wall, as shown in the middle left photo. If the wall has been painted, you might consider running the edge of a plastic putty knife around the edge of the fixture first to sever the old paint bond. This will help prevent any old paint that sticks to the fixture from damaging the exterior wall as the fixture is removed.

Disconnect the old wiring. Now you can locate the wire nuts for the old wiring and remove them as shown in the bottom right photo. Separate the wires and set the old fixture aside. Then remove the old mounting plate or strap that's attached to the electrical box and set it aside as well.

Install the new mounting plate. All new electrical fixtures attach to the electrical box via a mounting plate or strap. These are almost always supplied with the new lamp. Locate the mounting plate and attach it to the electrical box with the screws provided, as shown in the top photo.

Connect the new wiring. Before you hook up the new fixture to the existing wiring, there are a couple of things to do. First, if the new fixture requires any assembly, do that now. Second, since this is outdoors and exposed to the elements, odds are that the bare ends of the existing wires have become tarnished or corroded with age. Inspect your wires. If they are dark and dull or show evidence of corrosion (usually green or gray deposits), scrape the wires clean with a pair of wire strippers or a pocketknife. Now you can hook up the new fixture, pairing up white to white and black to black, as shown in the middle photo. Screw on the wire nuts to make secure connections. Then hook the fixture's ground wire to the existing ground or to the metal electrical box.

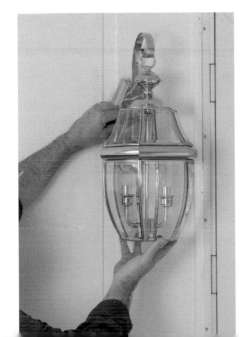

Attach the new fixture. With the fixture wired, you can attach it to the mounting plate. Make sure the wire nuts and electrical wires are pushed fully up into the electrical box. Then fit the fixture over the mounting plate and secure it with the screws or nuts provided, as shown in the bottom photo. Restore the power and check the operation of the light.

Index

METRIC EQUIVALENCY CHART

Inches to millimeters and centimeters

inches	mm	cm	inches	cm	inches	cm
1/8	3	0.3	9	22.9	30	76.2
1/4	6	0.6	10	25.4	31	78.7
3/8	10	1.0	11	27.9	32	81.3
1/2	13	1.3	12	30.5	33	83.8
5/8	16	1.6	13	33.0	34	86.4
3/4	19	1.9	14	35.6	35	88.9
7/8	22	2.2	15	38.1	36	91.4
1	25	2.5	16	40.6	37	94.0
1 1/4	32	3.2	17	43.2	38	96.5
1 1/2	38	3.8	18	45.7	39	99.1
1 3/4	44	4.4	19	48.3	40	101.6
2	51	5.1	20	50.8	41	104.1
2 1/2	64	6.4	21	53.3	42	106.7
3	76	7.6	22	55.9	43	109.2
3 1/2	89	8.9	23	58.4	44	111.8
4	102	10.2	24	61.0	45	114.3
4 1/2	114	11.4	25	63.5	46	116.8
5	127	12.7	26	66.0	47	119.4
6	152	15.2	27	68.6	48	121.9
7	178	17.8	28	71.1	49	124.5
8	203	20.3	29	73.7	50	127.0

mm = millimeters   cm = centimeters